MW00635140

Brass into Gold

Francesca Malloy
with Ursula Paes

A 2 Z Press LLC
bestlittleonlinebookstore.com

Printed in the United States of America
A 2 Z Press LLC
PO Box 582
Deleon Springs, FL 32130
bestlittleonlinebookstore.com
sizemore3630@aol.com
440-241-3126
ISBN: 978-1-954191-91-4

Alas! regardless of their doom,
The little victims play;
No sense have they of ills to come,
Nor care beyond today!

Thomas Gray, 1770

Dedicated to

Kerry Kathleen Malloy

"Many daughters have done virtuously,
but thou excelliest them all."

Contents

Illustrations

Introduction

Part I — Ursula's Story

1. Awakening 1
2. My Father 3
3. Starting School 7
4. Middle School 13
5. Teenage 17
6. WWII Begins 19
7. Surviving the War 25
8. War Ends, Atrocities Exposed 29
9. First Love 33
10. A New World 37
11. Central Islip 41
12. A Broken Heart 45
Postscript 49

Part II — Francesca's Story

Foreword 57
13. First Date 59
14. Little Nomad 61
15. Rock Valley 65
16. Culture Shock 75
17. High 79
18. Sixteen Dancing Darlings 83
19. Finale 89
20. Treason 93

21. The Milk Man 95
22. What's My Line? 97
23. Ursula and Lamb-chop.................................101
24. Junior High 105
25. Life's Saddest Times 111
26. All Over 113
27. Movin' on Up...141
28. Breukelen...157
29. Vend-etta 173
30. A Night on the Town....................................177
31. The Diva 181
32. Brass into Gold 185

Acknowledgements

Illustrations

Introduction
Ursula as a child in her winter coat, circa 1926
Map of Estonia, rendered by Kerry Malloy

Part I
6, Old Thomas, guardian of the city of Tallinn, the
    logo of the capital of Estonia
8–9, Article about the Estonian language
20, Map of Russians overrunning Estonia (*Between
    Giants*, Prit Buttar)
47, Ursula in her winter coat, circa 1990
48, Easter card from Ursula to Francesca
51, Ursula with a goat
52, Ursula with a macaw
54, Article about Ursula from Estonian newspaper
    Järva Teataja

Part II
58, Francesca and mother in Brooklyn, circa 1923
60, Francesca on the farm
64, The bungalow in Long Eddy
66, Francesca and Aunt Margaret harvesting Swiss
    chard, circa 1936
67, Arrowheads found in Rock Valley
69, Top: The Rock Valley Brook; Bottom: Francesca
    and Florence with water wings, circa 1929
71, Etta Kett paper doll (Paul Robinson)
73, Barbecue grill?
74, Our Lady of Lourdes, Queens Village (Wikimedia)
76, Sisters of Our Lady of Lourdes parish
78, Lady's pocket knife

80, Francesca on stilts, circa 1940

81, Bayside High School cheerleading squad, 1939–1940

82, Roxyette banner from 1940 State Fair

85, Dancing Darlings featured in USO article from the September 12, 1942 issue of *The Saturday Evening Post*

87, Dancing Darlings doing the conga dance, same issue of *The Saturday Evening Post*

91, Four Dancing Darlings without makeup or costume

92, Map of Pohnpei

94, Frances Gaitings and Ensign James Michael Malloy, Jr. at St. Patrick's Church in Miami Beach, Florida on St. Patrick's Day, 1945

95, James Michael Malloy III, the "Milk Man"

98, *The Kiss*, Gustav Klimt, 1907–1908

99, Portrait of Daniel Gaitings from the May 17, 1936 issue of *The Long Island Sunday Press*

100, Top: Invoice from Joseph Madison, 1913; Bottom: 1920s touring car

103, Fourth floor of The Towers, Jackson Heights

106, Postcard of shrunken men, The National Museum of the American Indian

107, Reverse of postcard

108, The National Museum of the American Indian housed in the Custom House, The Battery, Manhattan (Wikimedia)

110, The Malloy children: Kerry Kathleen, Sean Paul, Tracey Marie, Roark Anthony, and James Michael Malloy III

112, Mother's Day card from Kerry

114, Statues at Abu Simbel being moved (Wikimedia)

116, Statue being raised from the sunken city of Heracleion (The British Museum)

118, *What's a Bullet when the Heart's On Fire?*, Ardeshir Mohassess

120, Cappadocia (Adobe Stock Images)

121, "Ironing Ladies" sign, Ireland

122, Loch Ness Monster article from the September 5, 2023 issue of *The Epoch Times*

123, Stone Age settlement Skara Brae, Mainland Island, Orkney Islands (Wikimedia)

125, Toreador poster

127, Top: Little money used by Chinese workers; Bottom: Money used by the rich and foreigners

130, Little hand-carved rocker made of horn by a Cuban artisan/vender

131, Monument to the Rosenbergs, Havana, Cuba

133, A "house" in Tierra del Fuego (*Uttermost Part of the Earth*, E. Lucas Bridges)

134, Stone Age statues found in Malta depict bulbous women

136, Rotunda of Sanctuary Basilica, Malta (Wikimedia)

137, Mosaic of women athletes at the Villa Romana del Casale (*Piazza Armerina*, Officina Grafica Bolognese)

138, Monumento a los Niños Héroes (Monument to the Children Heroes), Mexico City

139, Postcard from Victoria, Canada

142, Old English sheep dog (Adobe Stock)

143, My 200-year-old Brooklyn house

148, Marly Malone jewelry

151, Roadster MG (Cars.com)

152, Corner building being stabilized

153, Corner building after brownstoning

155, Top: The carriage house; Bottom: Closer view of the stained glass windows

161, Soldiers' and Sailors' Arch, Brooklyn (Wikimedia)

162, Brooklyn Public Library

163, Top: *Fading Scroll*, El Anatsui (Joanne Mattera Art Blog); Bottom: *Rain Has No Father*, El Anatsui (Denver Art Museum)

166, The Prison Ship Martyrs' Monument, Fort Greene Park

167, Brooklyn City Hall, rendered by Lily Frances

168, Map of Brooklyn

170, Postcard of the Brooklyn Bridge with the Twin Towers beyond

171, Opening of the Brooklyn Bridge (Shutterstock)

174, 7th Avenue flea market

175, Artwork in acrylic and silver, painted by Dolores Tramontano

178," No Parking" sign, Brooklyn (Flickr)

184, Ursula and Francesca in Prospect Park, Brooklyn

185, Graham Home for Old Ladies

187, Angel of Grief, Greenwood Cemetery, Brooklyn (Wikimedia)

188, Ursula's photography in Prospect Park

189, Ursula in Prospect Park

190, Ursula enjoying "The Gates" by Christo, Central Park, 2005

191, Postcard of Mount Dora, by Tamla Maddox

193, Cake for Francesca's 100th birthday

Introduction

One hundred years ago, a little princess was born to a wealthy family on the other side of the world in a tiny country on the north coast of Europe, Estonia. 59 days later a little urchin was born to a poor seamstress and truck driver on the other side of the world in Jamaica, Queens, New York, USA. The Estonian child had four sisters, fine clothes, a governess and lived in a grand house. The Queens girl had no siblings, none of these luxuries, but had a mother who spoiled her with all the luxuries penny tips of a provincial waitress could buy. Twenty-two years went by and World War II erupted in Europe. Estonia was seized by the Russians and the princess's family was splintered around the globe. The urchin suffered a different upheaval when her parents divorced and her father died when she was eleven. She had no sisters and no brothers.

The war drove the American girl into an early marriage and drove the Estonian girl to flee to the USA. When they were thirty-three, they happened to meet in a night class in college and became friends and remained so for sixty-five years. They had divergent lives, one a scholar fluent in German, Russian, Estonian and English, the other a housewife and mother with no education.

Ursula as a child, circa 1926

PART I

(unedited)

1

Awakening

This autobiography is written for many reasons but mainly for its therapeutic value, to take stock at the crossroads of my life and, last but not least, that I may, by chance, be remembered.

Before going into details, I want to map out the crossroads at which I find myself.

One of the most shocking realizations is that I will soon be 39, not very old really, but an age at which one should know the directions one's life ought to take — and I am not sure at all. The other one is that I will have to decide what I want to do professionally because the grant under which I was getting my M.A. is running out and I will have to go to work again. The third realization, the one which makes all the others so urgent, is that after seven years of going steady or whatever one could call it, the bubble has finally burst and all my hopes and dreams for a family and an ordered life have come to an end.

Up til a short time ago, I had the illusion that once I got my MA, I would also get an MRS and settle down to a life of service, not to humanity but to my husband.

Anyway, this is not going to happen and therefore I hope that by looking at myself, what I was, and what I am, critically, I might be able to see my way a little more clearly and decide on a course of action that will lead somewhere where life will be bearable.

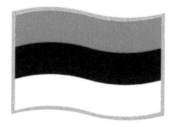

2

My Father

My father was the youngest of six children of a rather poor manager of a large baronial estate. He spent about six years in school and then went to work. I do not know what he did first, but eventually he, too, became manager of an estate. Later he went into some kind of business connected with horses and shortly after the First World War he bought a flour mill, a small textile plant, and heaven knows what else. By the time I was born, he was 32 years old and one of the richest men in a small town of 8,000.

My mother was the third daughter in a family of five girls and a latecomer boy. My maternal grandfather was a Swiss cheese-maker who migrated to Russia where he married a young widow of German descent. He later went to Estonia, then a Russian province. He was killed when a chimney collapsed and left his widow and six children. The youngest was barely six. My grandmother had a difficult time but all children received a high school education and at least half of them were headed for the university, although eventually only one really made it. The others all married and forgot about having a profession. At the time my mother married my father, she was working in a pharmacy preparing herself for the entrance examination for the university. As she tells it now, things were not going well at all, the only brother turned out to be a real juvenile delinquent and it was necessary to get a man into the house. So, she got married. She never said she loved my father, only that she felt sorry for him because he had lost his first wife in childbirth a short time ago. Anyway, she married him and in a reasonable time, I turned up. She said that the first years of the marriage were very unhappy ones. My father was extremely jealous — she was barely permitted out of the house nor could she talk to any men at all. Besides this, he felt that she was after his money and therefore never gave her enough for anything. Since by that time he owned a bakery and a small grocery store beside the mill she did not have to buy much. But money was a perennial problem — he always felt she would ruin him, and she never had enough for anything — clothes for the children and herself, gifts for the holidays for the employees and household help. It must have been a trying time.

When I was one year old the family moved into a fairly big house near the mill and the bakery. The house was situated at the edge of town, near a little river. On the other side of the river were the orchards, the stable for horses, the cow barn and behind them meadows, fields and further moors and woods. This was the one real home I ever knew and I can still remember it quite clearly, the shabby furniture, the sensible dull food, the cats, dogs, ducks and chickens, but best of all I remember the little river, the brooks running between the meadows which were also the boundaries of father's property and the woods.

I do not remember anything about the first years of my life except what I was told. Though an ugly little thing, my mother felt I was the most beautiful of all children, and father, whom I resembled to the point of it being funny, was also very proud of me. Since I was the first child in the family and all my friends were adults, I too was a little adult, well-behaved and quite serious. The greatest trouble I gave my parents, really my mother, because I was my father's only when I was good, was that I cried for about two hours every evening. When asked why I never answered. Sometime later one of my mother's sisters managed to find out what bothered me. "Nobody loves me." The family thought that this was the funniest statement of the century and haven't stopped laughing about it yet.

One day, it was a beautiful sunny day, the snow was still high, when I returned from a walk with my Russian governess, and I was taken upstairs. There in a big laundry basket, lay two bundles — the stork had brought me twin sisters. How this affected me I do not remember either. I only remember that when strangers threatened to take the babies away, I was always very upset, even though this became a routine procedure with the same people.

*Old Thomas, guardian of the city of
Tallinn, the capital of Estonia*

3

Starting School

When I was four, I went to kindergarten. I think I liked it a great deal because I made nice things and some of the other children did not make them so nice. The lady who ran the kindergarten moved away after a short time and I was back home playing with my dolls. Then the pastor's wife opened a kindergarten for some time — I was enrolled there too and again had a very good time, especially because I was praised for my clean hands. I must have been quite a respectable little snob in those days. I would return home from kindergarten and tell my father how good I was and how bad the others were. At that time, I also started to make my first money. We learned all kinds of poems by heart and I would catch father in his study in the evening and recite the poem to him. He would be very pleased and give me five or ten cents. When I tried to fool him and repeat the same poems after some time, he would only give me a penny. Life must have been quite good in those

THE ESTONIAN LANGUAGE

The ancestors of the Estonians arrived at the Baltic Sea 13,000 years ago when the mainland glaciers of the last Ice Age had retreated from the area now designated as Estonia. The first settlers who followed the reindeer herds came here from south, from Central Europe. Although the vocabulary and grammar of the language used by people in those days have changed beyond recognition, the mentality of the tundra hunters of thousands of years ago can be still perceived in modern Estonian.

Language and lingering mentality

Even the most ordinary everyday Estonian language contains numerous ancient expressions, possibly going back as far as the Ice Age. The Estonians say *külma käes, vihma, päikese, tuule käes* ('in the hand of the cold, rain, sun, wind'), or *ta sai koerte käest hammustada* (literally 'he was bitten from the hand of dogs' i. e. 'he was bitten by dogs') or *ta sai nõgeste käest kõrvetada* (literally 'he was stung from the hand of nettles'). Quite obviously, nobody any longer thinks that the wind, rain, dogs or nettles actually have hands. But in ancient times the moving, often personified natural phenomena, to say nothing about animals and plants, were believed to have certain powers. These powers, sometimes exerting control over human beings, were symbolised by a hand. Hence the contemporary Estonian *käskima* ('to order'; can be translated 'to give orders with one's hand'), *käsilane* ('handyman').

In all the above Estonian expressions 'hand' occurs in the singular. This is associated with the integral concept of the world of our ancestors. Everything formed a whole, a totality, also the paired parts of body which were used only in the singular. If one wanted to speak about one hand, one had to say *pool kätt* ('half a hand'). Hence the division of the holistic world into the right and left halves, right and left sides.

Even now, Estonians find their bearings spatially by using parts of the body, mostly without being aware of it themselves. If something is *kõrval* ('beside', 'next to'), an Estonian speaker does not even notice that what he is actually saying is that something is 'on his ear' (*kõrv, kõrva* meaning 'ear' and suffix -l corresponding roughly to the English preposition 'on'). The Estonian postposition *peal* ('on') means literally 'on the head' (*pea* 'head' + -l); *juures* (*juur, juure* + -s which corresponds in modern Estonian to the English 'in' but in earlier times stood for 'near' as well) means that something or somebody is close to the speaker's *juur* ('root'), i.e. the place where he touches the ground.

The majority of European languages belong to the Indo-European language group (e.g. Spanish, Polish, Lithuanian, Norwegian, Albanian, Romany, Greek or Welsh). Of the ancient European languages, once so widespread throughout the continent, Basque in the Pyrenees, the Finno-Ugric languages in the North and Central Europe, and Caucasian languages (e.g. Georgian) in the southeastern

The Estonian language belongs to the Finnic branch of Finno-Ugric group of languages. It is not therefore related to the neighbouring Indo-European languages such as Russian, Latvian and Swedish. Finnish, Hungarian and Estonian are the best known of the Finno-Ugric languages; rather less known are the following smaller languages of the same language group: South Estonian, Votic, Livonian, Ingrian, Veps, Karelian, Sami, Erzya, Moksha, Mari, Udmurt and Komi, spoken from Scandinavia to Siberia.

The relations between languages can often be seen from the similarities in numeric systems:

Estonian differs from its closest large related language, Finnish, at least as much as English differs from Frisian. The difference between Estonian and Hungarian is about as significant as between German and Persian.

Along with Icelandic, Estonian is at present one of the smallest languages in the world that fulfils all the functions necessary for an independent state to 'perform' linguistically. Teaching, at both primary school and university level, is in Estonian; it is also the language of modern science (molecular biology, astronomy, computer science, semiotics, etc.). Estonian is used in the army, in the theatre, aviation, journalism - in all walks of life. Estonian is the only official language in Estonia in local government and state institutions.

Estonian is spoken by approximately 1,100,000 people throughout the world. About 950,000 of them live in Estonia, and more than 150,000 are scattered over Sweden, Canada, USA, Russia, Australia, Finland, Germany and other countries. The first attempts to describe the Estonian language scientifically were undertaken in the early 17th century. In 1803, a lectureship of the Estonian language was established at what was then the German-language University of Tartu, founded in 1632. With the spread of the ideas of Enlightenment, the interest of the Baltic German Estophiles in the local language and culture increased. During the 19th century, the first educated Estonians began publishing scholarly research of their mother tongue. The first doctor of the Finno-Ugric languages of Estonian origin was Mihkel Veske who did research into the history of the Estonian language in the 1870s; the Estonian Writers' Union, established in 1871, undertook the task of standardising the common language.

In 1919, a professorship of the Estonian language was established at the University of Tartu where Estonian became the language of study in the same year. At present, research on the Estonian language-related topics is being carried out at the Institute of the Estonian Language in Tallinn, at the University of Tartu, at the Tallinn Pedagogical University, the Estonian Institute of Humanities, and at various research institutions all over the world.

Free Estonian Word -

early years, so much to do and not a worry in the world. In summer mother would pack up her daughters and go to my grandmother who lived in a seaside resort town. Two of my aunts, each had a boy, would come there too and we spent summers playing in the sand, bathing and getting an occasional ice cream cone. Never once did we get enough ice cream — one of our wildest wishes was to be able to gorge oneself on bought ice cream. There were many people around in these summers, grandmother's friends, mostly Russian ladies who used to come and drink tea with her; classmates of my mother and my aunts, sometimes even their former teachers would be met on the street or on the beach. These grownups would exchange all kinds of fascinating memories and exclaim about our rapid growth. Sometimes we would go visiting to play with the children of these classmates.

When I was six, I started Russian lessons. Mother thought the language beautiful and we had always had a Russian governess. But now the time had come when I had to learn to write and to read the language so that someday I would be able to read *Anna Karenina*, *Crime and Punishment* and all the other masterpieces in the original. I liked the lessons and was proud to be able to read. Usually, I was taken to and from my lessons, but when nobody had time, I was expected to come home alone. My teacher lived about five minutes from our house and there was no traffic to speak of in town, so it was really an easy assignment. The difficulty arose when two dogs were let loose behind a high fence in a garden that I had to pass on my way home. When the dogs saw anybody passing by, they started to bark wildly and run up and down behind the fence. Although the fence was high and sturdy, I was deadly afraid of them getting out. I would start howling louder than the dogs and run home at an amazing speed. Those were days when I used to cry my head off, not only because I was frightened of the dogs but also because nobody loved me enough to remember to come and pick me up after my lesson. I was still not going anyplace alone except in the yard, the garden or the street between the mill and the house. When I was seven, I started going to the real school. One of my mother's sisters whose son was about my age moved to our town. She had her apartment in the house next door. Since her husband had tuberculosis and political inclinations and therefore spent most of his time either in a sanatorium or in jail, she had to take a job to earn a living.

My cousin and I were the only pupils in first grade. We learned to read in no time and enjoyed ourselves immensely. He was not as good in arithmetic as I and, since I had no sense to go slowly, I would do many more exercises and, at the end of class when he had to catch up with me, I would sit there and wait for him to finish and come home. We both loved to read and would hide with our books where nobody could disturb us. While in first grade I also fell in love. Sometimes I think that this was the greatest love of my life, so far anyway. The boy was in the sixth grade, had black eyes and dark hair, was the greatest mischief-maker in school; and his family background was rather hazy. Since he did not pay any attention to me otherwise, I spent the next four years annoying him as best I could. Summers thereafter were in a way terrible because he went away someplace and I could not see him until fall. I used to spend hours thinking and dreaming about him — how we would have children and be married, I must add here that in those days I still believed in the stork and did not even suspect that there was anything resembling the facts of life.

In school, things were going well. After Christmas, another boy joined our class and in the fall another cousin and another boy came. I was the only girl in class and had become a real tomboy. The boys from my class and some older ones would congregate almost daily, weather permitting, in our yard or very near to my home to play cops and robbers. I was a quite respected member of this group because I could run as fast as any of them, and fight as well. When I was in third grade and an accomplished fighter and soccer player my sisters also started school and I had to take them with me when going to play. Since they were twins and very cute, they brought out the manly feelings in my friends which made me very jealous. But I bore this stoically, like a man.

Looking back on the first four years of school I think that they were very happy days. I was a good student, I had achieved a certain status in the group, and I had a very good friend in my cousin with whom I dreamt and fought, and made up and plotted against the tyranny of our parents, whom we found rather unbearable, especially my father who wanted what he wanted and almost everything he wanted seemed unreasonable.

4

Middle School

The summer after finishing fourth grade we were shipped to a different place for the summer. We went with our governess and stayed with an aunt whose husband was a Russian. This was to improve our Russian, because being out of the house a great deal more now that we were in school, we did not speak the language as much as mother wanted us to. So, we spent the summer with my aunt and uncle, played with Russian children and improved our accent. I remember this summer quite well not only because the resort was much nicer than the one, we usually went to but because our uncle used to take us out occasionally for coffee and cake, something which never happened at home. Also, this summer I got the news that I was to change schools in autumn. This was a great shock to me. The elementary school I had attended was a German school and I was not sure how I would manage in an Estonian school even though I had spoken the language all my life. And of course, I would be away from my secret love. The only consolation I had was that my cousin was to go to the other school too.

Coming home at the end of summer, I made friends with a girl whose family had moved into a house quite near to ours. This child had lived all her life in the capital city and was much more sophisticated than I. What she saw in me I will never know, but when I went to school, I had a friend who sat with me — we had double desks, and it was a declaration of friendship to sit together. The first few months were quite difficult. There were 45 children in class. I had become used to being one of six. I often did not understand what the teacher said, my spelling was so bad that I could not understand what I had written, nor could anybody else. My cousin was no better off and we suffered together. Things must have been pretty bad because we even got some help with our homework, a thing that had never happened before and was never to happen again.

But slowly things improved and, in the second year, we had established ourselves not only as some of the better students but also as members of our respective groups. I became friendly with some girls and my cousin with some boys — gone were the days of cops and robbers. The separation of the sexes had started and was to continue. The next six years that I spent in that school now seem also to have been rather happy days. I loved school and did well in nearly all subjects. Because my mother had failed physics in high school, I tried to duplicate this but fortunately did not succeed. I fell wildly in love with the history teacher — history had always been my favorite subject so it was a happy coincidence to have a male teacher for history. Most of the teachers were women, some of the strict

14

and some not much so, but that did not matter too much, since most of us were brought up to respect authority. I also learned to dance and attended every school dance that took place, there were no others, I think, in my sleepy hometown.

Once we got a new chemistry teacher. She was a bit dull and not a good disciplinarian. And it was soon rumored that she did not notice anything. So, during our first chemistry test, I came to class with a palm full of organic chemistry formulas. Everything went well so I grew bolder. For the next test, I came prepared with a better crutch, a piece of paper with nearly everything I could not remember on it. I am glad to say now that I got caught. But when it happened, I was ready to die!

These things were usually told to the advisor, the parents heard about it and it was usually a scandal that nearly made headlines in the town's semiweekly newspaper. How I was spared all this I will never know unless I have an opportunity to return to Paide and talk to the teacher who is still teaching chemistry there. Anyway, being a coward, I did not tell anybody about it, and nobody spoke to me about it. What father would have done if he had found out is too awful to think about even now.

5

Teenage

During this time, I started to develop an intense dislike of my father, he was stingy, he was inconsistent and he did not understand me, etc, etc, etc, etc. I don't remember too much now because I have recently become very fond of him, but then I prayed that I would be sent away to school. My mother did not understand me either. This became especially clear to me when I was about sixteen. I loved going to the movies but mother felt it was not good for children to see too many movies. They gave a wrong picture of life and one would never be able to face reality. So, my dose was set at one movie a month. This was a terrible thing to do since there was no way of knowing what movies would play in the coming month and I might see one movie today and the next movie would be much better. So, one day when I had seen my monthly movie the week before and an especially good film was showing I persuaded my cousin to go to the movies secretly. It did not occur to me to do this alone and besides I was afraid to come home alone in the dark. He was willing and so we made elaborate preparations

— we got all dressed up to go skating but, instead, we went to the movies. I still remember the movie, it was so beautiful and sad, never have I seen anything like it since. Everything would have gone well but a colleague of my aunt, the mother of that cousin, saw us and quite casually asked how the children had liked the movie. This hit the dinner table like a bomb — my mother cried that I had betrayed her, papa was furious, and I have not been able to forget the affair to this day. I sulked for days, then I tried to make up with mother, we both cried and I stayed home from school for a day, playing sick and getting over the upset. Why I was permitted to stay home I do not know, but maybe mother felt that this had been very trying for me. I wrote a long dissertation in my diary about parents who by their narrow-mindedness drive their own children to doing things secretly.

Not long after this the war broke out and our whole peaceful world of restrictions collapsed and I could go to the movies as often as I felt like, but then I did not feel like going to the movies anymore.

Those were the major catastrophes of my early life. I was by and large dissatisfied with everything, restless, and did not know what I wanted to do when I got out of school. That I would go on to the university (there was only one in the country) was the only sure thing, what I was to study I had not the faintest idea. Sometimes I wanted to be a teacher and influence "young" minds but since I was so shy in front of a group that I could barely open my mouth this seemed a questionable project.

6

WWII Begins

So, the years passed and all of a sudden it was 1939, the war started and first slowly and then faster and faster Estonia was drawn into the maelstrom never really to emerge again. First was the Finnish-Russian war and some of the older boys ran away to join the Finnish army. Then the Russians felt threatened by the Estonians and to protect themselves demanded bases, and since nobody came to our aid, that is what they got. We started to see Red Army soldiers in the seaport towns. They behaved quite badly and were surprised at what they saw. This was only a foretaste of things to come. In June 1940 the Russians decided to liberate the Estonian worker and on a beautiful summer day they descended on the country like a swarm of ugly gray grasshoppers. There was great confusion because they set up their puppet government and went at the business of liberation with their customary vim and vigor. They also started to pass laws. Then they nationalized all private property, froze bank accounts, increased taxes on property taken away, set up a new class system

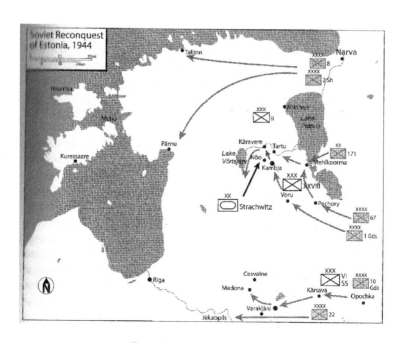

Russians overrun Estonia

20

and altogether made a mess of life. Anti-communist feelings became much stronger with the object of affection suddenly so close. There were rumors (based on fact) of sudden shootings, people being taken from their homes and never seen again, nightly visits by the secret police, and everything one can read in the American papers twenty years later.

Even though father had always tried to make us believe that we lived on the brink of bankruptcy, now we were really poor. We were permitted to live in only a few rooms of the house, the rest was empty. We had to pay immense tuition fees because father had been a capitalist. The salary he was getting now for running his business was taxed so heavily that we had about a ruble to live on. Father's only brother who supposedly had invested heavily in gold and buried it someplace dropped dead of a heart attack. There were rapes, suicides and everything to make a good Italian movie.

To make the confusion complete we all started to have scarlet fever, I was the first and when I was ready to go back to school the twins got it and when they got over it, it was the turn of the little ones. I forgot to mention that when I was thirteen, we had another baby and in two years one more — both girls.

Anyway, while things were going from bad to worse my father decided to leave the country, as did thousands more. Germany at this time was collecting all its nationals and bringing them back. Since grandmother was of German descent and we had attended the German elementary school somehow or other we managed to get out. We all had only one desire to get away from the Russians as soon as possible. So, at the beginning of 1941, we left our country and our home. We spent some time in a camp and then one of my aunts who had come to Germany earlier took me in. Since her only son, that favorite cousin of mine, was in the Navy, one of my life's greatest wishes came true — I found myself an only child. I enrolled in the last grade of high school and though everything was rather strange to me, the language also giving me some trouble, I managed to graduate but with an extremely mediocre record. This annoys me to this day but I guess I will have to live with it. After graduation I was at loose ends again but since the war was on and an awful lot of suffering all around, I decided to go into medicine. When I think back now how easy it was to get into medical school, barely any questions asked, I am still amazed. After the first semester, I had to work in a hospital where I caught diphtheria which kept me out of school for the next semester. I did not have a very good time during my student days. I did not meet anybody, and as before my favorite pastime was to dream of the day when some male would fall wildly and passionately in love with me.

All around was death and destruction. Bombings, victories, defeats, and everything becoming more insecure daily. The Russians were gaining steadily and it seemed more and more futile to have left everything and run away. As they had promised us when we crossed the border, they were going to get us anyway, wherever we were. The great Red Army would conquer the world, so why run?

Besides dreaming of love, I was also dreaming of death, of dying soon and young. I even set the date when the Lord was going to take me. But like everything else in my life it did not happen. I had not planned carefully enough and obviously, God either forgot our date or he had better things to attend to. So I just kept on hoping but I never set a date again.

After I had finished the second semester, had cut up a nice corpse and altogether started to feel like an old pro, the law was passed that all female first and second-year medical students were to interrupt their studies and go back to work. The end of the war was coming and things were very bad in Germany. The Russians were quite close now and people were starting to try to get away from the eastern border. I was assigned to be the nurse for two forced labor camps. People were assigned to dig ditches to hold back the Russian tanks. Most of the laborers were Poles who hated the Germans violently, did not like the Russians anymore, and were hoping that the English or Americans would descend from heaven and save them from both evils.

I kept office hours twice a day, gave out medications, diagnosed, treated, and kept people sick as long as possible. When I did not trust my own diagnostic abilities, I took my patients to another colleague, the village doctor, for consultation. My chief helper was a middle-aged Polish count, a painter in private life, who announced that he had *tabes dorsalis* and therefore could not work. After having looked up this word in the dictionary and being impressed by the diagnosis and the charm he used to convince me, he became my assistant, my chief translator, doing almost nothing but keeping public relations good. He also kept me informed about all rumors of Russian approaches, English-American leaflets, and other strictly "verboten" information. But too soon were the ditches in that area dug and my lovely sickly camp disbanded.

7

Surviving the War

I was reassigned — office nurse to a woman doctor miles and miles away from civilization. As lucky as I had been before with the people I had to live and work with, so unlucky was I now. The doctor was a singularly cold, distant person with whom I could establish no relationship. There was nobody else around but a Polish maid who, of course, did not particularly like me. Beside this it was November, there was no fuel, the house was cold, the outhouse far. I had to take care of the stove in the office and the fire would never start. The food was miserable too. I felt like a slave. And to top all this the Russians were coming closer and closer. Preceding them were the refugees who arrived in freight trains, wild terror in their eyes. Helping to unload them we would often find dead among them mostly the very old or the very young who had not withstood the cold and misery.

One weekend in January (1945), my boss sent me with an empty suitcase to the city to get some potatoes I owed her. I had kept my room there because I hoped to return and go to school again. When I arrived there, I found out that the city was being evacuated. The more important people had left already, there wasn't an office or store open, everything was in turmoil. I met one of my campers who invited me to stay with her, she would take care of me regardless of who came. But because I already knew the Russians I declined as politely as I could, grabbed a blanket and not much else and got on the last train leaving the city.

I did not know where to go nor what to do. I wanted to join my parents but was afraid that they had either also taken to the road or else had been caught by the Russians. I remembered that our former family doctor was head of a hospital near Berlin so I went there. One evening, while he was sitting in his office, the good doctor was surprised to find me standing before him, quite dejected, asking for a job as a dishwasher. He was very good to me and installed me in a nice warm room. I was fed, could take a bath, wash my clothes and work as a nurse aid.

This did not last longer than about ten days, then the Russians were there too and I was on the run again. I stopped off at a classmate's in Berlin to catch my breath and contemplate what to do next. I had been so used to doing as told that it was very difficult for me to realize that there wasn't a soul who could tell me, and what was worse there wasn't anybody who cared either.

Since I could not stay in Berlin, nor did I want to, I decided to surprise one of my university-time friends whose parents lived in Bavaria, far removed from the Russian threat, and rather in the way of the American armies. With the help of two soldiers who hoisted me headfirst through a car window, I managed to get on a train leaving for Munich. In Munich, I was to change trains and go on. When I arrived in Munich, I started to have doubts about going to see these people whom I had never seen before and whose daughter might not have arrived home yet.

Therefore, I went to the Red Cross which assigned me to a military hospital in a little town on the Danube. I took myself there and started to work. I don't think I ever worked so hard in all my life, nor will I ever, I hope. Trains were coming in daily with wounded from all fronts, they all needed care. At night we were often awakened to carry our patients into the cellar because of an air raid. It was incredible. But it probably kept me from cracking up. I did not know where a single member of my family, none of my friends or relatives were. I was in a daze. I worked and worked but when somebody stopped me to ask about my family I just cried. But people were very good to me. My charge nurse, a nun, gave me pep talks and tried to convert me.

After finding out that I was neither deaf, dumb nor an idiot, even my coworkers started to treat me kindly. Because they spoke a different German dialect and I could not understand them they had arrived at the logical conclusion that I was not all there. And for the first time in my life, I had lots of admirers. Of course, they were a semi-captive audience, but wherever I went in the hospital I usually had a shadow and sometimes more. Depending on their age and inclinations, they were either fatherly, brotherly or else. I, in turn, was motherly, daughterly or sisterly, I never quite reached the or else stage. I learned a great deal there and I think I was a good nurse, running over with human kindness. But I did not know how to make a bed with the patient in it.

8

War Ends
Atrocities Exposed

As expected, one day the Americans arrived. The war was over. Nothing much changed except that there were all the temptations that came with chocolate, cigarettes, and nylon stockings. But because nobody tried to tempt me, I stayed as innocent as ever. At the age of 22, I hadn't been kissed yet. I thought that at least this last deficiency had to be made up before too long, but I did not quite know how to go about it. All around me, girls were having babies, legitimate and illegitimate ones, and I was having terrible trouble being kissed.

Quite suddenly one lovely morning American ambulances by the hundreds turned up and before lunch the hospital was empty, every patient had been removed to a bigger hospital.

Before they left, I managed to have myself kissed — in the bishop's garden under an apple tree. The young man who did me this service wasn't really so young, he was 34, an age I was very fond of in those days, and an artist so I assume he knew what he was doing, but I was terribly disappointed. So, this was kissing, the thing books were full of! If I hadn't been so well brought up, I would probably have asked him whether he had done it properly. I did not say anything, I just thought that now we were engaged and he would come back soon to marry me.

I stayed in that town for a while, starved without being on a diet, and contemplated the general misery of life. After I got unbearably hungry and my funds had run almost dry, I went to Munich again to look for a job. I was sent to a TB sanatorium for former concentration camp inmates. The idea of TB did not appeal to me but since I did not know what else to do or where to go, I started to work there.

This was a huge place, formerly it had been Air Force barracks but now this UNRRA had taken it over and was trying to cure as many survivors as possible. It was amazing how much food was available there. The poor patients were stuffed with everything that was good for them, but they had no appetite. Even the staff was well fed and, in a short time, I was so fat that I nearly became too big for my skin.

Once I had eaten my fill, I started to look around and what I saw was more than upsetting. I had always thought that the Germans were not too bad, how could anybody who fought the communists be? My eyes were opened in a most cruel fashion. Though the patients had been cared for in the hospital for about five months when I came, most of the ambulatory ones were still so weak that they crept around hanging on to walls. The situation was indescribable and I do not want to recall it too clearly. There was also a lot of other mischief going on, rapes, prostitution, black-marketing was the favorite sport and any of the aftereffects of the war was there intensified by the fever of TB. Still being a great dope, I only found all these things out after I got married and my husband tried to educate me to the facts of life.

At the time I had my own problems of conscience, and being lost in the world and nobody to talk to I kept out of mischief. I was amazed that so many elderly gentlemen pinched my cheeks and asked me whether I was still a virgin. Being one, I did not catch the implication and treated them as dear old uncles and, after some time, they started to treat me like such.

The hospital was occupied much in the same proportion as the concentration camps; mainly with Jews, Poles, Greeks, Italians, and a number of other nationalities. The lovely prejudices, of course, flourished healthily on like in the good old days and a poor nurse had to be extremely careful with whom she spoke too often, with whom not enough, whose bed got made first and whose she made last.

I managed to be diplomatic and not openly prefer any side but since there were more educated people among the Jews this became increasingly difficult. We had two fourteen-year-old Jewish boys on the ward who elected me as the chief target of their need for love. Among two nuns, an elderly short-tempered German nurse and an orderly they really had not much to choose from. They were sweet boys, but they often embarrassed me in front of the nuns, who did not appreciate seeing their nurse being hugged and kissed by young men who would have to shave in the near future.

9

First Love

Among the patients on the ward, there was a young Jew from Hungary. His condition was very bad, he had to be tapped every week, he was tall and thin and one of those that crept around hanging on to the walls. And he was emotionally extremely unstable. When a patient whom he did not like was put into his two-bed room he promptly took an overdose of sleeping pills. But he talked about art, music, theatre, beauty, love, and nature. And what had to happen happened. I fell wildly and madly in love. Forgotten was the man who had kissed me under the bishop's apple tree, forgotten everybody else. One day I was asked for my very first date and although I did not know how to handle this I managed to accept. On February 22nd, 1946 we met in Munich and went to a concert of the Munchner Philharmonic where Hans Knappertsbusch conducted Beethoven's Third. Coming back on the train we missed the station and had to walk back about five miles through the snow in the middle of the night when the civilian population was not permitted on the streets after eleven. I must admit we had a beautiful romance. This type of man knows how to make the most of love — all the joys were heavenly and all the suffering hellish. I had waited for love all my life (23 years) and I was afraid that this was my last opportunity. So, we had our ups and downs, trials and tribulations, fights and reconciliations. And everything exaggerated to the nth degree. How I ever managed to rise to all those heights I'll never know.

Meanwhile, my parents had been found, I had heard that my favorite uncle had been taken by the Russians, my aunt had been raped by a band of Russian soldiers, brutally beaten and had calmly walked over the frozen bay until she came to the end of the ice where she stepped into the water. My parents and sister had also been captured by the Russians but were alive. So, I was not quite so much a feather in the wind anymore.

I was so carried away by my love that I wrote to my parents telling them that it had finally happened to me. My mother, without any hesitation, wrote me a very upset letter asking how could I get involved with a Jew. This upset me very much and I pretended to have dropped him. My parents were in Switzerland by this time and as far as I was concerned, they were in a different world.

My good friend was becoming more upset as time went on, one day he could not live without me and the next he calmly explained that poverty was the death of the soul and love, and if we stayed together being so terribly poor, we would kill love and soul. I, of course, felt that nothing could kill my love nor my soul, but being the shy type always agreed with anything.

One lovely summer day when we were sitting on the grass on the side of a street, he asked me to marry him. I accepted and as soon as our papers were straightened out, a process helped along with a pack of Camels, we were duly married in the town hall. Afterwards, we took the overcrowded streetcar to a café where one could have some reasonably good pastry and ice cream for our wedding breakfast. Afterwards, he went to earn his daily bread and I went home to wait for him and cook dinner. When he came home, he was in deep depression and did not eat a bite but lay on the bed staring at the ceiling. And so, life went — sometimes deep depression, sometimes elation. Fortunately, we had lots of friends who felt sorry for me and gave me some support when I needed it most. After having been married for a month, I let my family know about it and the whole Estonian community had a terrible shock. I became very bitter and refused to have anything to do with my countrymen; with my parents I kept up a lukewarm correspondence.

Shortly after my marriage, my husband's TB started to act up again, he handed over his job to me and took off to a sanatorium. From that time on until a few months before coming to America, he went from one place to another. I visited him there because he missed me so, or he would come home for a few days. I sat home, wrote him long letters and dreamt of the day he would be home for me to spoil and take care of. These were lovely days, and yet so sad. We had only one horrible room, the landlady hated my guts and denounced me where she could. How I ever survived it all and still kept my sanity I can't tell. But I stayed sane until my beloved returned. And then my real trouble started. He could not bear the thought of being married to me. He loved me he swore but to be married was worse than death. And look at me, I was ugly, stupid, I blushed without provocation, I did not know how to behave, what to say, etc, etc, etc. I agreed with everything, but that he did not want to be married to me nearly killed me.

10

A New World

Fortunately, our emigration was coming closer and we had to start packing and breaking up the one-room household. This kept us busy and he had not enough time to pick on me. Meanwhile, our mutual friends were giving me psychotherapy telling me how much better off I would be without him, and that even though he was crazy he was a nice boy and he really loved me.

He had a scholarship for a university in Ohio but what I was going to do was not settled at all. Finally, everything was done, x-rays taken, oaths sworn, going away parties given and attended and we found ourselves in what I hope was the last concentration camp — the DP Debarkation Camp in Bremerhaven. There everything was verboten for immigrants. It was a sad and humiliating experience for the future free citizens of a free country.

On a cold and nasty April day, we were put aboard the General Blatchford. Since the sexes were strictly separated on that ship, I found myself sharing a cabin(?) with 200 other females, who had nothing in common but their sex. Everybody was very happy, the food seemed unbelievably good and plentiful, and we all retired for our first night aboard ship with the secure feeling that we were finally, really and truly to leave Europe and head for the Promised Land. We had hardly left Bremerhaven when a storm blew up, and it kept blowing for nine full days. The poor General Blatchford became a ship carrying nothing but wretched creatures who were all sick, sick, sick. Since the DPs themselves were supposed to do most of the cleaning and keeping the ship in order, I cannot describe what shape that ship was in after one day of nearly universal seasickness. On May 4th we landed in New York. The morning was grey and cold, no trace of the famous skyline in the fog only the Spry and Maxwell House coffee signs on the Jersey side indicated that we had arrived in America. Customs inspectors searched through our measly belongings and the Salvation Army was there with coffee and donuts. Because we had no relatives or friends meeting us, somebody from HIAS came and deposited us in a most wonderful hotel, the Alexandria on 103rd Street. Our room had a private bathroom and we felt quite overcome by all the luxury. Last year I did my public health fieldwork in the area around the hotel and when I told my instructor that this had been my first American residence, the lady could only look at me in disbelief, such a horrible place! But I still remember the Alexandria with fondness even though I was seasick that first night on terra firma.

We looked up a few friends within the next days and started to contemplate what we would do to find a job. I had heard from my relatives that many

Estonians were working in Mount Sinai Hospital and decided to try there too. Although I had had quite some experience, I found out that this did not mean anything here. But Mt. Sinai took me anyway and promised to pay me $95 a month. I thought I was rich with that income, but found out only too soon that it was too much to die and too little to live on. My husband had found some kind of job with a photographer. HIAS had put us out of the Alexandria and we found a furnished room in a Kosher home. This room took the lion's share of our income and gave me a great headache because I had to pretend I knew about Kosher and not upset my old landlady.

Work was rather unpleasant; I had been assigned to a ward whose head nurse was famous for her beastliness not only to poor foreign ward helpers but also to student nurses and resident doctors. My duties were purely menial, dust, give ice water, wash glasses and bedpans. When patients were calling for bedpans, I was permitted to relay the message but not hand over a bedpan myself. Since I was much more sympathetic then than I am now I was extremely frustrated and disliked being unable to really do anything for the patients. Since I had been told that changing jobs in America was the thing to do, I started to look around for something else to do. One day I found an advertisement in the New York Times looking for a nurse aide in a camp for handicapped children. I had my interview, was accepted and managed to land a job for my husband in the same camp, too. After six weeks of working in Mt. Sinai, I said goodbye to the people there who felt that I had behaved very badly leaving so soon. I sympathized with them as best I could and took off for Camp Oakhurst. Besides putting some money in our pockets, the camp turned out to be a very good experience. We met a number of very nice people, made friends and really polished our English. We learned to say "ain't" and "hi" and whatever was fashionable in the summer of 1950. Autumn came only too soon and my husband took off for Ohio and I stayed in New York to look for a nursing school. I looked up a few hospitals in the phone book and started to make rounds, being sure that they were all waiting for me to do something about the shortage of nurses in America. On that pilgrimage I had a few sad surprises — in New York Hospital the tuition was about $1,000, in Bellevue I could put my name on a waiting list, in Mount Sinai they wanted only eighteen-year-olds, and, in St. Luke, they did not believe in breaking up a Christian marriage. I was at the end of my wits when a kind lady in St. Luke's got on the phone and found out for me that, in some state hospitals, the semester had not started yet. She made an appointment for me with somebody who made another appointment for me with Mrs. McLaughlin in Central Islip.

11

Central Islip

I appeared there and apparently touched that lady's heart for when school started on September 19th, I was there even though my papers were still being processed in Albany. Everything turned out for the best, they accepted me and I was very happy to have a roof over my head for the next three years, and three meals a day. I liked being a student and I had a very good time. All the restrictions that bothered the younger kids didn't affect me because I had nowhere to go and nothing to do but study. Every day I wrote my husband a postcard and every day I got one in return. Since we were apart love was blooming again and we dreamt about being together. Vacations would give us an opportunity and, after a few days, he would start to complain again of the sad fact of being married. But it was not too bad and I hoped that everything would be well someday. When I started my last year in Central Islip, Steven started a one-year course in physical therapy in Columbia, having received a scholarship from the Polio Foundation. I used to come home to the apartment he shared with a friend on weekends. We saw each other more often and our relationship started to deteriorate again. He accused me of being ugly, dull, stupid, etc, etc, and all I could do was agree and cry. Then he would feel sorry for me and we would have a tranquil time for a while. After his graduation, he went to North Carolina on an assignment because they had a polio epidemic. I had to stay behind to finish my last year of school.

As soon as he was out of sight, he started to miss me terribly. Why weren't we together, what did we have in life but each other, and here we were so far apart. I was trying to keep my head and was looking around for a job in the city, but as could be expected, after an especially beautiful letter I weakened and, since school was over for me too, I took a bus to North Carolina and we were together once more.

Things went quite nicely in Asheville. We did a lot of hiking, got our first car and enjoyed life. But this was not to last. By Christmas '53 we were in New York again, in the same apartment, with the same friend. I worked at University Hospital, took courses at NYU, cooked, kept house and suffered. Things were getting very bad. He often challenged me to leave him, or he promised to go himself. When I could not take it anymore, I rented a room near the hospital and, one night when he had celebrated a friend's birthday by imbibing too much, I packed my bag and cleared out. Since he knew where I worked, he showed up there the next day and wanted to know why I had made him suffer so terribly. He had awakened at five in the morning and not finding me had been unable to go back to sleep. And, since I had left him, would I mind being his mistress if not his wife. He would always love me in this case. Since I was much more interested in being a wife than a mistress we had a few more arguments on this theme, but generally, we saw each other seldom. He sometimes invited me to the theater or for dinner to the apartment but what I was waiting for, an invitation to come back and stay, never came.

Finally, I went out to Albany and got a divorce and never saw that man again. Friends kept me informed about him, he married very soon after the divorce, stayed married for a short time, and then married again. What has happened since I don't know.

12

A Broken Heart

I had always believed in eternal love, and when I found my marriage on the rocks, I was very upset, to put it mildly. I felt that all my life had come to an end and that there was really nothing left to live for. But as in most such cases I too got over my grief and disappointment and in due course fell in love again. But I tried to be smarter this time and picked a man who appeared the opposite of my husband, he was short, blond, bald, Christian, and seemed to know what he wanted. He was also very middle class. And I thought that if he fell in love with me, he would be married in no time. But soon I found out that marriage was not to be very soon because he had a million troubles, and other responsibilities, etc. But he LOVED me. Being in love myself, a patient dope, and trying to be understanding I kept loving and hoping.

Every time I went home to see my parents, I hoped he would greet me on my return by saying that I would never leave him again; every time there was a turn for the better in his undertakings, I hoped this would be it. Every time I suggested we part because later it would be more difficult, he found reasons why we should not, but what I was waiting for never came. He was unable to ever make a clear statement and even though I knew what that meant I did not have the strength nor the courage to draw the consequences and act accordingly.

Finally, early this fall when I was starting my last term in school, I got him to admit that he could not think of entering into a childless marriage. He wanted to have a reason for living, and the only reason was a child. I nearly had a nervous breakdown, but knowing that I just could not afford anything of this kind I have been dragging myself along. I cannot think of anything but him and me. I don't know what to do, should I leave the country, should I do this or that. And I have to be sensible because whatever I do now will make a difference later. I have one more course to take for my degree so I cannot go too far, and if I got too far, I will have no place to come back to. If I pull up my roots in New York I will be completely rootless. My head will not reach the clouds, nor my feet the ground.

I have to find a job to give me enough satisfaction to make up for my present state of mind, but it also has to be a stepping stone for professional advancement. But more than anything else would I like to go and hide someplace until I have collected my wits and am ready to act sensibly.

This is my life up to now.

Ursula, circa 1990

MMXIII

Dear Fran!
Wishing you
very happy
Easter
and
Joyfull Spring!

Love

Note the date

48

Postscript

In 1956, I first met Ursula. We were students at NYU in night school. We were 33 years old. By 1983 we were old friends and spent many hours in museums, art galleries, concerts, the ballet and theatre. No opening went undetected by Ursula. She kept abreast of the arts and devoured them all. She had several friends, divorcees, spinsters, and widows; there was always someone available to accompany Ursula while she tried to satiate her hunger for culture. Ursula also liked good food. We dined in New York's finest restaurants. Her tastes were continental. She savored escargot as an entrée, and sweetbreads to follow. If a fish was served whole such as branzini she ate the head first. She shunned cocktails but liked wine with her dinner.

For over 50 years, she lived in a top-floor apartment of a lovely brownstone townhouse built in the nineteenth century on a beautiful block in Park Slope, Brooklyn. The stairs were formidable. As she aged neighbors carried her groceries up the four flights for her and lovingly referred to Ursula as "a national treasure."

It was a short walk from Prospect Park and Brooklyn Botanical Gardens. When she was not pursuing the arts in her free time she was enjoying the pleasures of the fields, flowers, streams and rose arbors in the park. At other times she would surreptitiously slip into the toddler's playground in Brooklyn Heights to sit and watch the little ones toddle, play and battle with each other.

Her appearance was ordinary. She was neither

fat nor skinny. Her clothes, conservative, good quality, slightly worn. Ursula had a wry sense of humor. She made you laugh but she herself never laughed nor did she smile. She made humorous remarks, always with a serious expression as though she did not realize she was being amusing. But she knew well that she was.

Ursula never used bad language, spoke of others in a detrimental way or stooped to gossip. She was very proper. Her mind was on finer things.

Ursula remarried in 1963 to Voldemar Paes.

Ursula did go on to earn her bachelor's degree at NYU and became a registered nurse. She started as a school nurse for the NYC Board of Health and advanced to the position of District Supervisory Nurse for the Public Health Services Administration in 1973. Her job was to visit doctors and hospitals to instruct them in the latest medical advance in the 1970s, which was family planning. Ursula was an atheist, did not attend church and was an advocate of birth control.

Although never having had or wanted children of her own, she was very proud of her nephew who left Switzerland and relocated to Japan to study cooking.

Her husband Voldemar died in 2000 and Ursula was left alone. She cared and cooked for herself. On holidays she would bake favorite Estonian cakes and cookies topped with hazelnuts.

Although she could no longer carry groceries up the four flights of stairs, Ursula was able to go up and down to fulfill her desire for culture.

Someone handed Ursula a goat

She continued taking courses at night at Hunter College and visited museums and art galleries in the days. When not in class, her evenings were filled with concerts, the ballet and theatre. New York City was the perfect place to satisfy her hunger for culture and the fine arts.

While living in Brooklyn she visited her parents in Switzerland. The rest of her family was spread over the whole world, from America to Australia.

Finally, when Ursula could no longer climb the stairs to her apartment, she retired and moved to Bradford, a small town in Western Pennsylvania, home of her youngest sister Gertrud, her only relative in America. In Bradford, she moved into an assisted living facility.

Era photo by Francie Long

Chapel Ridge resident Ursula Paes appears to hold a conversation with "Toby," a Red-Fronted Macaw. They have a few things in common, matching colors and "expats" from foreign lands. Ursula is originally from Estonia. She came to the United States in 1950 and settled in Brooklyn, N.Y., where she eventually studied nursing and worked in hospitals and healthcare facilities for many years. She moved to Bradford to be near her sister, who resides in the city.

Those were not happy days for Ursula because the other residents were local people who, for the most part, had never heard of Estonia. There were no cultural places or events nearby and the other residents tended to stick together since they were locals and were former schoolmates. Ursula had no chance of meeting anyone near her level of education or knowledge in that small town. She was very lonely. Her sister Gertrud was widowed and was very busy caring for her daughter Sophia's three children, so did not have much spare time for Ursula.

From Bradford, Ursula kept in touch with her Estonian roots. In 2016, she read in *"Vaba Eesti Sõna,"* an Estonian newspaper, that folk dancers from Paide were coming to perform in Westminster, Maryland, sister city of Paide, Estonia, Ursula's hometown. She contacted the troop of dancers and remotely followed them on their tour and gave consistent encouragement. In 2017, the mayor of Paide sent her a gift, a statue of Paide Vallitorn (the ruins of a castle tower in Paide).

Ursula died in Bradford on September 19, 2019, at the age of 96. *Requiescat en pace.*

Paide fänn Ameerikas heldis linnapea kingitusest

Hiljuti äsutis Ameerikasa Pennsylvania osariik asäkeses Bradfordi linna Paide linnapea Siret Pihelga saadetud kingitus – krivist Paide Vallitorn. Selle saaja Ursula Simson Paes on suur Paide fänn, kellele läks kulmagaust andsiannust linnast saadetis väga südamessa.

Ursula Simson Paes süllesunduk Paidesti saadatud kingitusesse.
Foto: Paides

KOMMENTAAR

Article written in Estonian about Ursula

54

PART II

Foreword

We cannot go back in time. That is too bad because a lot of good has gone like water under the bridge. Our food, for one thing, has been destroyed forever. Cross-pollination cannot be stopped and genetic "advances" be reversed. Yes, the strawberries are big and luscious looking and the carrots are perfect in color and shape. That is where the dream ends. Produce is tasteless. Onions no longer make us cry. They have lost their zap. Fortunately, our children do not know that their food is pap and that their meat has been altered so that swine grow as big as cows and chickens bigger than turkeys and neither taste like pork or chicken. No amount of seasoning or herbs can replace the succulence that has been bred out of everything we eat — but who remembers? A few of us do remember but we are limited to four simple words to describe heavenly savors: salt, sweet, sour and piquant.

Next is clothing. Linen, cotton and wool are going the way of silk, becoming scarcer each year. Chemically made fabrics keep our bodies neither warm nor cool. They have, however, to be fair, reduced the price of clothing and everything else considerably.

The world has changed in so many ways in one hundred years. We think we cannot live without airplanes, television, computers and cell phones. May God preserve us from nuclear war or an earthquake.

Brooklyn, NY   1923

13

First Date

I was born in the Roaring Twenties. My mother was a "flapper." She danced the Charleston and wore dresses with fringe and above the knee. Mom was a divorcee and in her twenties. One night she had a date but she did not have a babysitter so she took me with her on her date. I was about five years old. We went way out to farm country on Long Island to an old dilapidated farmhouse. It had unpainted clapboard shingles and a porch barely above ground level. The windows and door were covered with heavy drapery on the inside and it was very quiet — until we opened the door. Inside, besides the air being heavy with cigarette smoke, the walls were vibrating with loud conversation and laughter. We entered and looked around for a table, or at least some chairs. The place was packed. My Mom and date ordered a drink at the bar and ginger ale for me. We drank and left the place that was once called a "roadhouse" but was then known as a "speakeasy."

Prohibition lasted until 1933, the year that my family all crowded around a tiny radio to listen to the election results. Hoover lost his bid for a second term in the White House due to the terrible depression and his failure to deliver on his promise of "a chicken in every pot." Franklin Delano Roosevelt won the election and remained President until I grew up and married. He died in office April 12, 1945.

Francesca on the farm

14

Little Nomad

In 1928 we were so poor that my mother had to ask her friend, Irma, to take us in. Irma and her husband, Lee, were poor dirt farmers in Delaware. They kindly shared their poverty with us. I was five years old and a city kid. I picked some burrs and made a perfect straw hat. Some imbecilic grownup said, "Now put it on your head." I did. Then to remove the hat my head had to be shaven bald.

My first recollection of school was in the third grade. Mrs. Brown had a long stick with a rubber tip. It was called a pointer and she pointed a lot. We had no books but there was a wooden rack in the front of the room similar to one that holds a comforter at the foot of a bed. Hanging on the rack was a giant book, the pages made of oilcloth. It was about 36" x 36", old, faded and wrinkled. The large print ran perpendicular to the binding. On the cover were the words "The Three Little Bears." Mrs. Brown would aim her pointer at one word at a time and the class would read the words in unison, "once" "upon" "a" "time." When the story was finished, the pages were flipped back and we would start all over the next day. By the end of the semester (five months then) we could all read.

One lunch hour I spent my pennies on bubble gum. I chose yellow from the three colors, red, blue and yellow. There were two thick slices, enough to choke a horse. I put the whole package in my mouth and savored the sugar and lemon flavoring. By the time I got back to class, I was chewing a wad the size of an unbaked loaf of bread. Mrs. Brown told me to remove the gum from my mouth. I obeyed. Then she directed me to place the blob on my nose. There it stayed, to my humiliation, until dismissal. The punishment had its effect. To this day, I do not chew gum and look upon those who do with disdain.

In fourth grade, my mother was called to appear only once because of my behavior. It was the fourth school I attended because we moved every year. My mother would rent a furnished room from a family that would watch over me from 3 p.m. to 5 p.m. while she was at work. This fourth school was built on the city limits. We, my cousins and I, walked over furrowed fields on abandoned farmland. On the way, we passed a scary place, isolated and forbidding, called Creedmore. To make matters worse there was a murderer on the loose who left his symbol at the scene of his crimes, 3X. The boys, to capitalize on this drama, would write in chalk "3X" to frighten the girls. The crimes were never solved, the killer never caught.

Creedmore was one of three insane asylums built by the State of New York on Long Island. The second was Brentwood in Nassau County and the third, about sixty miles from the city in Suffolk County was Central Islip. The same Central Islip Asylum at which my friend Ursula trained and earned her R.N. degree. In the 1960s there was a social movement against institutionalization of the mentally ill. The hospital in Brentwood was closed and then reopened under the name of Pilgrim State Hospital where mentally ill patients are still treated. Creedmore, too, is still operating as a psychiatric hospital. Central Islip, however, where Ursula lived for three years, is gone, demolished.

The bungalow

15

Rock Valley

From the age of six to the age of fourteen, I spent summers in the Catskills. It was a rural place, very rural. We had no electricity, no telephone, no refrigerator, ice, or car, but my family had "a summer home" a bungalow in the mountains. We played in the brook every day. Our toys were stones. We feasted on wild berries and learned the names of all the wildflowers. We caught trout by hand illegally and eel by hook legally. In the valley, there may not have been electricity, but we had billions of stars and could identify every constellation.

Before plastic was invented, flotation devices were usually made of rubber. However, we learned to swim in the brook with water wings. They were made of canvas. First you had to make them soaking wet and then you inflated them like a balloon. They worked for children but they did not come in adult size.

The nearest town to our bungalow in Rock Valley was Long Eddy, five miles away. It had one general store with a gas pump in front. The town also had a bar and a church. It sat on the bank of the

Delaware River and its opposite shore was in Pennsylvania. The railroad discontinued passenger service there one hundred years ago.

Imagine life without a refrigerator, ice, or communication to the outside world. We ate home grown vegetables, fresh fish from the brook and chicken and eggs from nearby farms. In the early days, the valley road was a dirt trail. It ran from the Delaware River to the top of two steep mountains, one ending at Basket Lake where we sometimes went swimming. At the lake, we caught frogs and brought them home for a treat of *cuisses de grenoille*.

Francesca and Aunt Margaret harvesting Swiss chard, 1936

Farmer Hughs, our next-door neighbor a quarter mile away, had a dairy farm. He let us, my cousin Florence and me, go up on the mountain to bring down the cows at the end of the day. Each cow had a girl's name and each knew her own stall in the barn. I thought that was so smart.

Before we tended to Bossie and her herd, we always checked the arrow high up in an old oak tree. The arrow was a precious remembrance of the early inhabitants of the Valley. Along with hand-carved stone arrowheads found on the ground among the rocks is all that is left of the people who inhabited that rugged land centuries ago.

Ancient hand-carved arrowheads found
among the rocks in Rock Valley

I learned to milk when I was nine. It is not as easy as it looks. First, you have to position yourself on a three-legged stool. I don't know why it only has three legs, but there must be a reason for making you so unsteady. Second, tame the cow's tail. Catch that swishing, tangled brush and tuck it between the milk bucket and your knee and keep it there. Rest your cheek on the cow's belly and find the udders with your two hands. Do not pull the udders and expect to hear squish squash in the empty bucket. You will get no milk by squeezing and pulling. Place your thumb and index finger about an inch above the udder and gently pull the milk down. Squeeze the top of the tit and work the milk down to the opening. You will have a cup of milk in an hour the first time but things perk up with practice. A draught of that warm, frothy, cream-rich raw milk can make you drunk with delight.

Berries are plentiful on the mountains. In season we went out like a patrol, four or five females dressed against the briers and sun would attack the sunny side of the mountain and collect raspberries, blackberries and sometimes gooseberries. Gooseberries are rare, they are green and have a translucent appearance and bristles. They are edible but scarce. Elderberries grow profusely along the brook and are harvested by the adults for wine making.

The Rock Valley brook is a sustaining feature for a wide variety of wildlife. The woods harbored foxes, wolves, raccoons, wildcats, woodchucks, bears and rattlesnakes. When we heard that *shshsh,* we ran for our lives. One summer there was a biblical invasion of grasshoppers. They crunched underfoot and jumped up our legs. The wildlife had a banquet that season. The brook was rich with trout and eels. Mountain springs gave us the purest drinking water and served as our refrigerator.

The Rock Valley Brook

In the brook, 1929
Francesca and Florence with water wings

Once a year there was a "social" at the Valley schoolhouse. The farmers' wives made chicken and dumplings, homemade bread and ice cream. Never, never would you ever taste food like that again but the memory lingers forever.

At night we played childish card games like Go Fish and Old Maid plus checkers and dominoes. Monopoly had not yet been invented. We played by the light of kerosene lamps. Kerosene was used for the stove as well. The stove worked similar to a gas stove with burners of flame. There was no nylon or polyester so clothes had to be ironed. Two irons made of cast iron were heated on the open flame. Then while one was in the hand with a potholder the other heated to replace the cooling one in the hand. Nylon was invented during World War II and was used for parachutes. Before that women wore hose of silk.

On rainy days, I played with my paper dolls. Sunday newspapers such as The Journal American had comics we called "funny sheets." Two of the characters were Etta Kett, a brunette and Winnie Winkle, a blond. They were in competing papers and I had them both. The figures were about six inches tall and suitable for cutting out and being pasted on cardboard. These were "paper dolls" and were very popular with girls from eight to twelve. I played with them for hours, designing outfits for all occasions, decorating them with my crayons and colored pencils. These were the precursors of the Barbie doll and in keeping with the time of The Great Depression.

We had a wind-up Victor Victrola with their logo, a little dog sitting next to a huge funnel-shaped speaker. There was an eclectic collection of records from pop to opera. Enrico Caruso, a famous operatic tenor, gathered dust while we danced to "When the Red Robin Comes Bob Bobbin' Along." The records were about ten inches in diameter and were made of wax. Thomas Edison, the man who invented the light bulb, also gave us the phonograph. When I was eight years old, I read his obituary in the newspaper and I remember it because the tribute mentioned President Lincoln. Edison was eighteen years old when Lincoln died, and it made me feel connected to the Great Emancipator and the history of my country.

There was no mail delivery in Rock Valley. Our address was simply, Long Eddy, New York. Zip codes were not even an inkling. On July 1, 1963, the post office introduced the Zone Improvement Plan (ZIP) code. There was no Rural Free Delivery (RFD) as there is now. We had to pick up our mail from the post office. But there was no post office. The mail was dropped off at the home of Mr. Bjorkland, the designated "mayor" of the town. There was a switchboard in his parlor and later, when the valley was provided with a party line telephone service, Mrs. Bjorkland became the one and only switchboard operator. There was only one line for the whole valley and if you picked up the phone and a conversation was going on you could hang up or listen in. If you wanted to make a call you had to wait until the line was free and Mrs. Bjorkland came on and said, "Number, please?" Then she would connect you to your party. There were no dials or keypads.

We often had a campfire going in the yard. Twigs and dry branches were plentiful all around us. "Charcoal," "barbecue," and "grill" were words absent from our vocabulary. We did not have hamburgers or hot dogs. Instead, we roasted potatoes by throwing them in the coals and while waiting for them, about 45 minutes to cook, we toasted marshmallows two or three at a time on a willow branch. We built our "grills" by building a wall of flat stones in a semi-circle about twelve inches high.

Barbecue grill, circa 1929

I don't recall ever seeing or needing a doctor in all the summers I spent in the valley. We had no vitamins, but there was a nasty liquid, cod liver oil, against which we rebelled. Chicken, fish and eggs were our main sources of protein. My beautiful, loving Aunt Margaret, my maternal grandmother's sister, boarded me as well as two other children for the summer, Anthony Rizzo, child of a family friend from Manhattan, and my cousin, Francis Rausch, occasionally. Aunt Margaret had three children of her own, Ellen crippled by the first horrible polio epidemic, Arthur, the middle child, and Florence, eighteen months younger than I, my playmate and someone to fight with.

When we became teenagers, our social life picked up. My mother, by this time, had a little Ford with a rumble seat. She would take us to square dances at least three times a week. We became so proficient that we knew which dance to perform at the first three notes from the fiddle.

Our Lady of Lourdes Grotto, Queens Village

16

Culture Shock

My fifth year of school was a bombastic shock. Courses in the public school in the fourth grade had been Nature Study (mostly birds), Music Appreciation and such. I was enrolled in a new school just built by Our Lady of Lourdes parish in Queens Village. Next to the church, near the rear end, and a block from the school, there was a grotto with a life-sized statue of Blessed Mother Mary. Every May 8th the school children would parade in a procession, sing hymns, and a favored student from the lower grades would crown the statue with flowers.

> Oh Mary, we crown thee
> ♪ With Blossoms today
> ♫ Queen of the angels ♫
> Queen of the May

We loved that day. It was a holiday for us — no school. Diagonally across the street from the grotto was a grand house on a corner plot, the home of Ruth Snyder, notorious for being the first woman to suffer capital punishment by the electric chair. Ruth attempted to murder her husband, Albert, seven times before she made the cut. She and her lover finally succeeded by employing a picture wire for garroting, chloroform and a sash weight for beating. They staged the scene as a burglary but they did not fool the men in blue who discovered some of the alleged stolen items still in the house. In the end, Ruth and her lover, Henry Gray, turned on each other before they went to the electric chair, she ten minutes before Henry.

Standing Sisters: BORGIA, MARY STEPHEN, VERACUNDIA, FELICITAS, ELISE, NICHOLAS, FLORENCE, HUGH FRANCIS

Sitting Sisters: PANCRATIA, ASSUMPTA, MARY DE LOURDES, ALMA, LICIA MARIE, ROSALIA.

The fifth-grade curriculum covered: English Grammar, Math (decimals, fractions and percentages), History, Geography, Civics, Music and Religion. After handing in their Math and Geography homework assignments, students stood when their name was called and recited, from memory, the whole history assignment, dates and battles of the Civil War, and later in the day questions and answers from the Catechism. What an awakening!

We played a game at recess and lunchtime where we flipped a jack-knife into a marked rectangle of soil. A line was drawn from border to border according to the angle the knife landed within the demarked box. The knife thrower claimed his territory in turn until the box was all used up. The one with the most land won. The point here is that in 1937, twelve-year-olds could, and did, bring knives to school. I was the only girl who played Territory with the boys. I always had my Official Girl Scout knife handy.

As I remember, in the 1930s and '40s folding knives, also called jack knives or pen knives, were very popular. There were two-inch knives for a lady's purse, usually of sterling silver or mother-of-pearl; three-inch knives of gold for a rich man's dress suit; and four-inch knives for real guys. Each end had a blade, one small, one large. After a while, knife makers became creative, putting additions such as a screwdriver, a bottle opener, a scissors or a nail file. Jack-knives became too heavy and bulky and went out of favor. After that, people became more lawless and jack knives *verboten*.

Every morning, after we saluted and pledged allegiance to our flag, we were inspected for clean fingernails and having a freshly laundered handkerchief. Of course, we wore uniforms and, of course, I was terrified of the nuns. I graduated four years later with honors. Unfortunately, I was sent to public high school and fell back to my errant ways.

Lady's sterling silver pocket knife

17

High

I was a school dropout. Well, kind of. When I was seventeen and in high school, I took a job as a chorus girl in my senior last summer. It was a troop that entertained at state fairs, the stage was usually set up in an arena or in front of race track bleachers.

The memorable thing about the job was that the producer had us walking on stilts for the final number. We were dressed in toy soldier outfits and strutted to a military march, one hand in a salute and the other by our side. There was no holding on. It was all a matter of balance. Thusly, we strutted in formation, eight girls on one-foot stilts, seven on two- foot stilts, and one brave girl on three-foot stilts. She did not march but came out at the end to take her place in the middle to form a tableau before we clack- clacked off stage.

Oxford-type shoes with laces were nailed to the stilts. Our feet were laced in. The hand poles were sawed down and leather straps attached that went around our thighs. Before we dressed the trouser part of the costume was placed on the floor with the stilts placed over the open legs. Prop men who tied our oxford laces brought the trousers up over the stilts so we could put our arms through suspenders to hold them up. Then the jackets and then the hats. The routine went in reverse to disrobe from the uniforms with the help of the prop men.

You were the captain of your ship for the terrifying fifteen minutes of the routine. You can imagine the relief when the last note sounded, the curtain went down and we were to be released from prison.

The summer job ran over into the school year for about a month. When I returned to Bayside High School, where my only accomplishments were: Secretary to the school newspaper (because I was the fastest typist in the class) and a cheerleader (because I knew the right people). These right people, however, did not help me when I appeared a month late for school. I had been cast off as a dropout and the administration would not let me back in.

Bayside High School Cheerleading Squad, 1939

In the picture, I am second from the left, kneeling, and my best friend, Muriel, is third in back of me. She married right out of high school, was stricken with Alzheimer's in her forties, and met a horrible death when she wandered out of her newly purchased summer home in the mountains of North Carolina and fell off a cliff. A helicopter had to be engaged to drop into a wooded gully to retrieve the last remains of my darling, sweet friend Muriel.

My dear stepfather, Norman Tallman, a renowned horse trainer at Belmont Racetrack — really knew the right people. He took me to see his doctor. We explained the situation and the doctor promptly perjured himself and wrote a note fraudulently claiming that my absence was due to illness. I was reinstated. I graduated with no honors and with what they call a "General Diploma," a designation for undistinguished dummies.

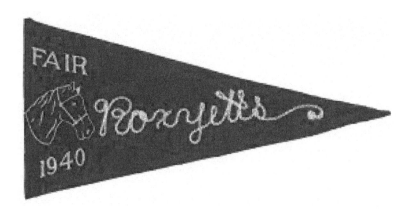

18

Sixteen Dancing Darlings

It was 1941. There were no jobs. All the high school graduates stood in long lines at one employment agency after another looking for work. Finally, I started as a record clerk for Sears Roebuck & Co. I worked five days a week from 9 to 5 and a half day on Saturday for a salary of $16 a week. Japan sunk our whole fleet in Hawaii on December 7 and we declared war on December 8, 1941. I quit being a record clerk and joined the USO (United Service Organization) as a chorus girl in a group assembled to entertain the troops.

During World War II, the United Service Organization (USO) put together several professional groups that entertained the troops here and abroad. Each group was comprised of a chorus line, a comedian, a master of ceremonies (MC), a couple of vaudeville acts, four musicians and a famous visiting star (actress, tenor and the like) who would spend two weeks with the troop. The musicians would rehearse with the military bases' orchestra in the afternoon and be ready in the evening to accompany our show with beautiful orchestral music. The chorus line was trained by the Roxy Theater in New York City where they featured the Gay Foster Girls, precursor to the Rockettes (Radio City Music Hall was not yet in existence). Besides dancers, the Roxy provided routines, costumes, a wardrobe lady and a manager who was a Gay Foster Girl herself. Our troupe was named "Sixteen Dancing Darlings." There were three dance routines for the line of sixteen chorus girls. The opening number was based on a popular song of the time, "The Jersey Bounce." The costumes, except for a little white blouse, were red with white polka dots. The short, full skirts barely covered the torso and we wore big, round-rimmed Madeline hats. We tap-danced, made formations and bounced large, very large, balls, in unison; the illusion being a group of young girls in a playground.

To assemble a chorus line the producers put an ad in a newspaper. In my day, it was "The Daily News." The ad was known as a "call." The chorus call gave the time, place, usually a theatre, and the name of the producers of the shows. Dancers would check the News every day if looking for a job. About a hundred girls would show up and all came prepared with tap shoes, leotards, etc. to show off their skills and their bodies.

First, the girls, already known to the producers from earlier productions, would be singled out and they would be the first chosen. The rest would be lined up and eliminations started before they could show their dancing ability. That is because a chorus line must be symmetrical. Those who were too tall, too short, too heavy or skinny were eliminated.

THE SATURDAY EVENING POST

September 12, 1942

Three things the Army likes best in shows, in the order of their popularity, are girls, girls and girls

The Jersey Bounce. I am third from the left.

Then dancing ability was tested. Basic steps were asked to be performed and agility for high kicking was necessary. The producers and dance trainers who were choosing could tell the quality of a dancer's work by her posture, the way she used her arms and hands and the way she held her head. Height was very important. The line of heads had to be straight, or with a gradual rise to the center. Size and dance skills were all that mattered. Facial beauty and tresses were of no importance because heavy stage makeup created unblemished skin, beautiful eyes and rich lips. Shadowing could simulate high cheekbones and smaller noses. It was all art. Hair was enhanced by all kinds of extension pieces, "falls," "rats," etc. While on stage, all girls wore flesh-tinted, fishnet hose to make their legs perfect. From the audience, the hose could not be detected and everybody's legs looked gorgeous. A lot of time and energy goes into making a darling chorus line.

After the girls are hired rehearsals begin. Ours was in the summer. There was no air conditioning. Salt pills were passed around. We practiced seven hours a day and learned the intricate tap routines. Then we had fittings and adjustments to costumes. We did not meet the rest of the cast until the first show in Watertown on the Canadian border.

We started in New York City and toured all the large military bases along the East Coast, Texas and then as far west as the Mississippi.

The show started with the chorus line, then there was a trained dog act with four little pups performing all sorts of impossible tricks. Next, was a classical guitarist who played melodious music that was sweet and soothing. Then, the MC announced the Sixteen Dancing Darlings again for another number with formations. This time the girls were dressed in short chartreuse boleros with enormous ruffled sleeves, bare-midriff and fuchsia satin tight pants with full bellbottoms. On each hip, the girls wore a tom-tom. They beat the drums in time while dancing the conga in formation. The eye-catcher in this number was on the chorus girls' heads. Each was wearing a sombrero forty inches in diameter. During rehearsal, while we were learning the routine steps, the formations and how to beat the drums in time, we had to practice with the hats on. At first, there were too many close encounters and hats were puddling all over the floor along with the blood from our tender hips being pounded for hours as we practiced the dance steps and had to play the tom-toms at the same time.

Sixteen chiquitas dancing the conga

Next came a truly great artist, a comedian named Joe McKenna. He performed alone and left the audience dumbstruck. His act was imitating a drunk. He would tell some jokes then slap his forehead with his palm, lean back and to the shock of the audience would keep descending backward with his feet glued to the floor until he laid on the stage flat on his back. Not to shock the ladies into a faint, he would rise and continue telling jokes. Before the act was over, he performed this incredible feat three times. That was a hard act to follow, but the dancing girls came on with a great finale to the show. It was an intricate tap dance to the Hungarian Rhapsody with the usual chorus line high kicks at the end. It always bought down the house. The servicemen, be they soldiers, sailors or marines, always reacted uproariously and riotously when the girls' arms joined at the waist and they let those legs fly up in unison and with precision.

19

Finale

It was a lovely evening and we were at a Marine base in the South. The girls were all in costume and the orchestra ready to strike the first note. We waited. We waited. It was pitch dark. The electricity at the base had failed. No light. We waited — in vain.

Finally, the enterprising marines took matters into their own hands. They rounded up every truck and jeep on the base and formed them into a semicircle pointed at the stage. At a signal from their commander, the stage was lit up with improvised footlights. These marines were not going to let a minor glitch like an electrical outage deprive them of seeing the Sixteen Dancing Darlings' high kicks. Semper Fidelis — the show must go on.

The show was over for that night, and three girls, still in stage makeup, went looking for an all-night diner, a cup of coffee and a breakfast bun. They did not get far before a police car pulled alongside and, refusing to listen to reason, threw the three Dancing Darlings in the clink and charged them with soliciting. The town was not known for its Southern hospitality.

Some window signs read "No dogs or soldiers allowed." So, no wonder it took a bit of persuasion for the US Government to help our manager spring the hoofers. Biloxi, Mississippi was the name of that unwelcome place where, even drawing a bath, was unpleasant. The water was sulfuric and had the odor of rotten eggs.

Louisiana, now that was an amenable place. Being Passover, when we reached New Orleans, a wealthy Jewish family invited some young army officers and a few of our girls to participate in their Passover supper. Muriel, our youngest Darling, met Leon, a US Army First Lieutenant. They fell in love. She was sixteen. Months later, as our Pullman car slowly entered the DC station in a downpour; a train coming from the opposite direction was also slowly advancing. It was an act of God. Muriel and Leon saw each other through the splashing raindrops on the windows of their passing trains momentarily as the cars pulled to a stop. Each ran out onto the tracks where they hungrily embraced. It was a scene from a Russian novel. After the war, they spent the rest of their lives together when Muriel Porselain became Mrs. Leon Dickoff.

It was hot in the South and our daily rehearsals and performances were debilitating. The job was not a walk in the park. It took strength, energy and grit. Texas is so large that we traveled for three days without seeing a hotel. We slept on the train; two in a berth — not because the USO or the USA were cheap, it was because all trains were requisitioned for the troops.

Only eight of us sixteen Dancing Darlings survived the road trip. The other eight, as well as the Gay Foster Girl manager, had to be replaced one at a time as they fell. We played at 72 camps in four months.

Four Dancing Darlings without makeup or costumes

St. Patrick's Day 1945

20

Treason

In 1945, on Saint Patrick's Day in Saint Patrick's Church in Miami Beach, I was married to Ensign James Michael Malloy, Jr. We shared a cottage with another honeymoon couple for a few weeks and were then transferred to the Princess Hotel in Key West where the waters were infested with barracuda and stingrays and the room with palmetto bugs. We dined on turtle meat almost every night. Other meat was rationed as were sugar, butter and shoes.

Then Mike was shipped out to the Pacific and I went home to wait for the war to end. We then committed treason. It was a military secret where the United States fleet was going to land. We devised a way that I could know where Mike had been sent. Instead of using V-MAIL, not quite tissue paper, six inches wide bordered in red and blue for airmail designed for overseas servicemen, I bought two 8 ½" x 11" world maps. We each had a map and stationery of the same dimensions. When he landed on Pohnpei, a tiny island in the middle of the Pacific, he marked it with a pinhole on his letter. I simply had to put his letter over my map and a crime punishable by imprisonment or even execution had been committed. All mail was censored but, lucky for us, the captain missed the pinhole. That little spot on the map, the Island of Pohnpei, is no longer in existence. The United States blew it up after the war in an atomic test. The evidence of our crime was obliterated.

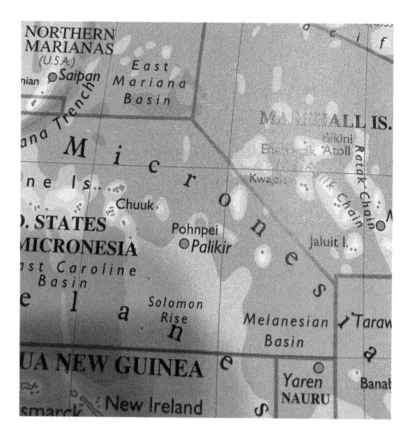

Mike returned home safe from the war and we settled down in Jackson Heights, Queens and, on November 16, 1947, a little blue bundle, Michael Malloy III, arrived; and he spelled trouble.

21

The Milk Man

The year was 1949. Before daybreak, milk was delivered to our apartment doorstep three times a week in glass bottles. On one of those predawn nights, an airline worker was returning home from the night shift at LaGuardia Airport. He entered the apartment building in Jackson Heights and, in the lobby, was met with a surprise. An eighteen-month-old toddler, who barely yet toddled, was wandering around alone in his baby blue Doctor Dentons. The toddler was James Michael Malloy, III, later known as Mike Malloy.

While his mother was in the hospital delivering his baby brother, Sean Paul, his father was in charge of James Michael, but it was 4 A.M. and dad was asleep. James Michael awoke and went looking for his mother. First, he went to the kitchen. No Mommy. He had already looked in the other rooms of the small apartment and she was nowhere. He could not ask Daddy, "Where's Mommy?" because he was not old enough to talk. Walk, yes, but talk, not yet. But the inability to speak did not stop the little brain from speeding along. The determined tyke dragged a chair ten feet across the dark kitchen, into the twelve- foot hallway to the front door. He climbed up on the chair, unturned the Seagal lock and unsecured the security chain. He opened the door, stepped out and tip-toed through the glass-laced wall of milk. He was exploring the lobby when the Good Samaritan from Pan American Airlines came in. Amazed, he took the toddler up to the 4th floor.

He rang Mrs. Zeigler's doorbell. It's now 4:30 A.M. Mrs. Zeigler has two little boys of her own so Samaritan thought Mike belonged there. She neither needed nor wanted another little boy, but she was very gracious and took him in. Shirley Zeigler was a good friend and neighbor. She took in the little waif, with whom she was well acquainted, and telephoned his father, James Michael Malloy, Jr. Half asleep and in disbelief, he jumped into his trousers and headed for the door. After tripping, and cursing over the chair left in the dark by his namesake, he opened the door and rushed into the lobby, knocking the three bottles to the terrazzo floor, creating a stew of broken glass and milk.

One Mike was too small and the other too big for spanking.

22

What's My Line?

In the early days of television, there were about five stations, all black and white. One of the major stations featured a popular program, "What's My Line?" A panel of three would question a contestant and try to guess his occupation. Dorothy Kilgallen, an investigative reporter, was the most popular on the panel. While she was exploring the assassination of President Kennedy she was murdered and found with her makeup and false eyelashes still on, propped up in bed. The murder has never been solved and was written off by the authorities as a suicide.

My paternal grandfather would have been an ideal contestant for "What's My Line?". He was a gilder. Who would have guessed that? A gilder paints in gold — real gold. The metal is pounded into a powder and spread thin on sheets. The surface to be gilded is painted with a liquid that stays tacky and is called sizing. The gold sheets are then pressed onto the sizing.

A famous painting by the German artist Gustav Klimt, entitled "The Kiss," is an exquisite example of the art of gilding. It is an oil painting highlighted profusely with gold leaf — painted in 1907.

The process is over 5,000 years old. When they carved figures in stone, the Egyptians painted the faces of their gods in gold. Thieves soon found a way to chip the stone and steal the gold. That, incidentally, is where we get the word "defaced," which means to blemish or disfigure.

The Kiss, Gustav Klimt

My grandfather had a lifetime job decorating the interior walls of Catholic churches. He used a stencil and applied the gold all around the interior of the church at about eye level with interruption only by stained glass windows and carved oak doors. Grandfather was a calm, gentle man and well-suited to his occupation. His father, my great-grandfather, Daniel Gaitings, fought in the Civil War and left a diary of his days as a soldier. The book, still in the possession of the family, is dearly treasured.

LONG ISLAND SUNDAY PRESS, MAY 17, 1936 — Page 8

Vivid Diary of a Jamaica Civil War Veteran

Daniel Gaitings

My other grandfather, Joseph Madison, Madison being an anglicized name from the Polish version, was a machinist and a millwright. Besides having his own shop he had a telephone in 1913 and he had a job. His telephone number was 2793 Beekman and his job was to keep the ferries running to and from Staten Island in New York Bay. True to his profession, he owned one of the first automobiles built, a touring car, made in the 1920s.

Telephone 2793 Beekman

New York, *June* 21 1913

M_ *H. Hinge*
Tribune Bldg N.Y.

TO **J. W. MADISON**, DR.

MACHINIST AND MILLWRIGHT

Repairing Paper Cutters and
Bookbinders Machinery
a Specialty

35 FULTON STREET

A 1913 invoice from my grandfather's business.

23

Ursula and Lamb-chop

After World War II, hundreds of thousands of deployed military men returned home and were looking for jobs. Fortunately, Mike's father had a friend who had a friend who was an insurance executive. He gave Mike a low-level job. The company insured several airlines so although it was not an aeronautical engineer's job it did have a tangential fit. As our family increased the pay did not keep up with our productivity, but Mike stayed with that company for the rest of his life.

It's hard to believe now, but in the 1960s I had an allowance of $54 a week to feed a family of six. I became quite adept at preparing meals on a shoestring and saving by such things as watering down the whole milk with reconstituted powdered milk. The Catholic meatless Fridays were a godsend.

It was pre-plastic times and we paid a deposit of 5 cents on glass bottles for which we would get a refund. One Friday, when my allowance was used up as it usually was, I was bringing my bottles for a refund when I tripped on a curb and fell. The bottles sang all over the street. I was eight months pregnant with Roark at the time. People picked up me, my shopping cart and my bottles, and sent me along my way. That tragicomedy was so embarrassing, though it was 53 years ago, I remember every detail. Pride makes it painful to be the object of pity.

Another unforgettable incident around that time in my life when I lived in The Towers in Jackson Heights, was the day a neighbor, a 50-year-old woman, who lived below me came to my door and asked if I had some sheets. I had lots of old sheets in the linen closet because I am what is called a hoarder. The woman was a professor someplace and I was in trepidation when confronted by her. She said she was locked out. She took the sheets and proceeded to the back of the apartment and opened the window. We were on the fourth floor about 45 feet from the ground. Then she tied a sheet to the foot of a bed and the opposite corner to another sheet, and then another and another until she had a billowy rope of cotton. Then, Mrs. Powerful said, "Don't worry, I did this before in Germany when I escaped the Nazis." I was stupefied at this proceeding and did nothing to stop this formidable woman. She climbed out the window holding onto the sheet and hand over hand lowered herself and with one hand opened her window on the third floor and climbed in. I don't remember having ever seen her again.

At that point in my life, a bit of gossip reached my ears. An erstwhile friend referred to me as a "drudge." My husband, Michael, graduated from Notre Dame with an aeronautical engineering degree. After serving in the war, he could not find a job.

The Towers, showing the 45 foot high 4th floor window

There was a horrible depression and airplane factories were closing. Mike used his GI Bill of Rights to go to law school. Now he was an aeronautical engineer and a lawyer and I was a drudge.

My fake friend's remark lit a bomb under me. We were sitting around the dinner table, Mike and me and our four children, Michael 9, Sean 7, Tracey 4 and Kerry 2, when I said, "I'm going to college." Mike said, "That's nice, dear." The children paid no attention. That week, I enrolled at New York University for my first course, Expository Writing I.

That is where I met Ursula and started a life's journey of 20 years in night school. Along the way, we were blessed with a fifth child, Roark Anthony. He was born on August 31st, so I did not miss one semester.

Ursula and I were the oldest in the class, older than our professor whom we code-named Lamb-chop. That was the name of a loveable puppet character on a popular children's television show. Ursula was born January 5, 1923, and I was born 59 days later on March 5, 1923. Two people could not be more unmatched, she born in wealth, highly educated, fluent and literate in four languages and an advocate of birth control. I, born into poverty, with my "general" diploma from high school, no knowledge of any language but English and, at the time, the mother of four children.

Every week, Lamb-chop handed back my papers folded and marked "C" or "D" and Ursula's papers with a smile on the brink of laughter with an "A." At the end of the term, Ursula earned and "A" and I was given an "incomplete." We had a conference, and Lamb-chop told me what expository writing meant. It meant that you had to quote an authority for everything you said on paper and make a footnote on the page with the name and work of the "expert." Original thought did not count so I made sure to plagiarize the second half and drew an "A" with a "B" to replace the "incomplete."

24

Junior High

I continued my night studies, became an English teacher and went to graduate school. But before they let me enroll at Hunter College I was sent back to high school (also night school) to take courses in Chaucer and Shakespeare.

At the junior high school, where I taught in Queens, I met some wonderful lifelong friends. The school was rough, the job was tough. We hung together and even our strict chairman grew proud of our accomplishments and claimed some of the glory. One of my colleagues, Tom Newby, was a truly dedicated teacher. He would sometimes give up his Saturdays to take his classes on an educational excursion. Tom was talented, had a beautiful voice and loved to sing opera. He was able to get the best out of any student who wanted to sing or dance or act. Every year he trained students after school and produced a Broadway musical. The results were miraculous. Middle school children, up to ninth grade, were turned into stars. They even built the scenery so if a child could not perform in the play he could draw, paint or do carpentry. The neighborhood loved these shows and looked forward to them every year. Thomas Newby, my dear friend, became a saint in 2017 at the age of 71.

We all took our students to museums, shows and exhibits. On one of the trips to The National Museum of the American Indian, which was located in Upper Manhattan at that time, we saw an exhibit of two shrunken men, one a native the other a Caucasian. Yes, real shrunken men processed such as heads were shrunken in New Guinea, but these were whole-bodied shrunken head to toe and propped up in a glass case three feet tall.

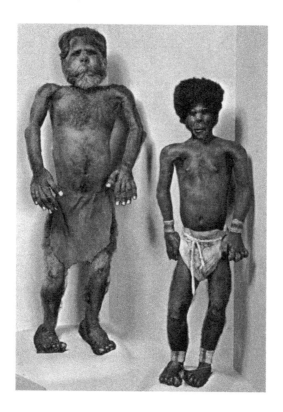

In 1961, Michael Rockefeller, son of once Vice-President Nelson Rockefeller, and great-grandson of Standard Oil's John D. Rockefeller, traveled to New Guinea in search of specimens of shrunken heads. At that time it was made known to the American public that some natives of the South Pacific engaged in the practice upon captured enemies and pictures of samples of the horrible practice were in the newspapers. Young Rockefeller was never heard from again. The irony of it was that we had two specimens right here in our own hemisphere.

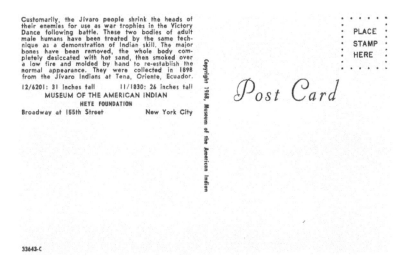

Customarily, the Jívaro people shrink the heads of their enemies for use as war trophies in the Victory Dance following battle. These two bodies of adult male humans have been treated by the same technique as a demonstration of Indian skill. The major bones have been removed, the whole body completely desiccated with hot sand, then smoked over a low fire and molded by hand to re-establish the normal appearance. They were collected in 1898 from the Jívaro Indians at Tena, Oriente, Ecuador.

107

The shrunken bodies in the Museum of the American Indian did not make it to the museum's new, scrubbed quarters in The Battery at the tip of Manhattan. I believe that the curators felt that they should censor the public from such a raw, dehumanizing exhibit which only they are privileged to see. Think of all the school boys deprived of their glee at actually witnessing an example of man's inhumanity to man. Had I not had the curiosity and surprise to prompt me to purchase a postcard at the museum, no one would believe this story.

The Custom House

In 1994, the Museum of the American Indian was absorbed by the Smithsonian Institute to the detriment of that primitive collection. It is now housed in the old Customs House, built in 1907 by the government as a place to collect tariff revenue on imports. It stands in Battery Park at the southern tip of

Manhattan. Gone is the comfort of the casualness of the old setting, replaced by formal exhibits under bright lights, marble and gilt. Many of the more primitive exhibits, including the shrunken men, have been shipped to Upstate New York for exhibition — so they say.

In the 1970s, I caught the Asian flu and nearly died. My thesis was due. I sent in 40 pages and my poetry professor sent them right back with a note: "You need 40 more pages." I persevered and was rewarded not only with an M.A. but was transferred to one of New York City's special high schools for gifted students, Brooklyn Technical High School, where young wizards are preparing to be architects and engineers and need to have proper English.

Clockwise from top left: Kerry Kathleen, Sean Paul,
Tracey Marie, Roark Anthony, James Michael Malloy III

25

Life's Saddest Times

In July, 1970, my beloved husband, Mike, 49 years old, succumbed to a heart attack. After 25 years of marriage, I was widowed and had five children; one already married and out of law school (the Milk Man), one in college, two in high school and the youngest nine years old. We somehow came through those years with the help of many wonderful people, relatives, friends and school administrators.

By the time, the youngest was in college, I had moved to Brooklyn and saw Ursula quite often.

On December 2, 2014, my dear, gentle Sean Paul lost the battle against heart disease and left us bereaved. Sean was a mathematician and a scholar. He taught Math at a small college on Long Island. When not teaching, he was reading and researching and his interests were boundless. Sean was a quiet man. We always thought of him as a loner. What a surprise then at his funeral there were more than 100 people. Sean, "We hardly knew thee..."

My sweet son, he will always be with me.

I'm proud of my children. They all stayed out of trouble and all graduated from college. Mike, a lawyer, has four children and six grandchildren; daughter Tracey, a lawyer, has three sons and two grandchildren; Kerry, the cartographer who graciously made the map of Estonia for this book, has three sons and one grandchild; Roark has three young children ages eight to thirteen. So, in all, I have thirteen grandchildren, Molly, Meghan, Moira, Michael, Zachery, William, Samuel, Ryan, Kelsey, Sean, Ilsa, Roark and Adelaide, and nine great-grandchildren, Patrick, Erin, James, Margaret, Anna, Marissa, Desmond, Rose Brooklyn and Lee Elvis.

While I rejoice and give thanks for these God-given gifts, Ursula is shaking her head in grave disapproval.

Thank you for
not selling me
to the gypsies.

Happy Mother's Day

From Kerry

26

All Over

My first trip abroad was to England because I only spoke English and I was afraid to venture out alone and not be able to communicate with other people. I was struck by the beauty of London. Why had no one ever mentioned that? Why do they not write about it? All I remember are complaints about the weather, the rain, except "I bring fresh flowers for the thirsty flowers" *Shelley*. When I left Heathrow Airport and was on my way to London, I was amazed at all the blooms, they were everywhere in all colors. Even in London proper there were window boxes, hanging baskets and pots all overflowing with flowers. The polished door hardware on every building large or small is a pride of the English people. Also, the palace, the parks, Westminster, the statuary and the architecture, especially on the curved road where the buildings were built in a convex line while buildings on the opposite side of the curved street were a solid concave line. To me that was amazing. The whole countryside was landscaped to perfection, everything trimmed, everything in bloom.

My next venture was the best tour imaginable — so good that it was discontinued, probably due to the company underestimating the cost. This was my choice was because the tour included Egypt and that was my main goal — to see the hieroglyphics. In Egypt, the tour included a boat trip, the boat being a Hilton hotel, down to Abu Simbel, which though being south is upriver because the Nile starts at Lake Victoria in Central Africa and flows north to the Mediterranean. Abu Simbel is a shrine where two gigantic statues of Egyptian gods were removed during the building of the Aswan Dam and then returned to their original place.

The statues at Abu Simbel

On the way, we passed a village where little boys came out in tiny boats made of oil drums. Each drum held one little beggar with a paddle. They were irresistible. We stopped at a village in Lower Egypt and took a short walking tour. A remarkable site was an old man squatting on the ground ironing clothes with irons heated on a small charcoal fire in a pot. He was gap-toothed which was important for his profession because he took a sip of water from a jug and squirted it out to dampen the cotton garments as he stretched them over the ironing board with his hands and ironed with his foot. This turned out to be not as unique as I thought because, later in the journey, I saw another man also ironing with his foot in the same manner.

In 1933 a Royal Air Force pilot, while flying near the Nile delta, noticed ruins in the water. His report started a long search for the sunken city of Heracleion. It was found about 5 miles off the coast from Alexandria only about nineteen feet underwater. The discovery prompted further research and in the year 2000, almost 70 years later, French underwater archaeologist Franck Goddio, with the help of modern sonar equipment, found the ruins he had been reading about in ancient histories and searching for over the years. The city is referenced in the writings of Herodotus and other ancient authors.

The underwater site is vast and may have been not one but two cities. Slowly, the ancient treasures are being raised and taken to Alexandria for preservation. There is a new museum in Cairo, the Grand Egyptian Museum, that exhibits some of the sunken treasures. But, if you happen to be in London,

Statue from Heracleion being raised

you can see some of these antiquities in the British Museum.

We had a short stay in Beirut, just long enough to enjoy a French meal for which the city is famous. On the way out of Lebanon, we saw a hillside covered with tents. Some had TV antennas that bespoke their intention of permanent residency. These were

116

Palestinian refugees who refused to go home even though differences had been settled with the Jews.

Because of unfriendly relations with Iraq, we had to have special permission to cross the border and stay a couple of hours under guard in Baghdad. The guards took us to a military museum and then to a hotel for lunch. The meal was more to Iraqi taste than American but we were grateful for the food. Goat meat stew made with yogurt was the main fare and green grapes that were overdue for dessert. The streets of Iraq had many people asking for money sitting on the curb with a hand stretched out, including women with babies.

We visited Iran and were free to travel around the country while the Shah was in power. The women in the capital city of Tehran all covered themselves with a large shawl called a chador. These are awkward garments, but the women have mastered them—one hand holds the hand of a small child while the other holds a shopping bag of groceries. The chador is kept in place covering the head and body by a small button sewn along the side which the woman holds in her teeth. I was appalled at this manmade disability. The one bright spot was that in Iran many of the chadors were of fabric printed with flowers. I did not see that in any other country. Tehran streets were bordered with ditches of running water so parking was perilous. Cars, however, were rare in Persia in the 1970s, but there were American soldiers with jeeps.

We traveled from Tehran to the city of Isfahan in Iran and stayed in a hotel with a pool. A young boy of about twelve was in the pool with us every day. He invited a few of the women to his home and we accepted his invitation out of curiosity. He acted very manly and insistent so we accepted. He took us to a lovely big house, ordered his brothers to disappear and then ordered his mother to prepare tea for his guests. His sisters were allowed to join us for tea. It is strict protocol in Iran that unmarried men and women may not socialize.

Chador covered women with makeup
by Iranian artist Ardeshir Mohassess

Another day in Isfahan was less pleasant. While a group of us were exploring the town, an old crone attacked one of our party, a young teacher from California, and started beating her to the ground. The reason for such a ferocious attack was that the girl was wearing shorts. It is understandable that a woman who had to wrap herself in a chador all her life would be shocked into insanity at seeing all that flesh exposed. A cautionary tale — check customs before you travel to a distant land.

After Iran, we headed for Greece and a cruise around the islands. Although the islands look close together on a map, they are not. It takes a day to sail from one to another in rough waters, rough enough to cause seasickness.

Once Byzantium, then Constantinople, now Istanbul, the capital of Turkey sits on the bank of the Bosphorus where one can dine on fresh fish at a restaurant on the shore while overlooking the water when you are not watching the belly dancer offered as entertainment. Americans also enjoy watching Kocek, twirling men dressed in long circular skirts, as entertainment but to Turks, it is a religious ritual.

There is much of interest to see in Turkey if you fancy historical places and peoples. The most famous tourist attraction in the capital is Hagia Sophia (formerly Saint Sophia) Cathedral/Mosque depending upon which religion is favored by the current ruler.

The tour took us to Cappadocia to see the caves carved from volcanic eruptions, there since the Stone Age and still inhabited today. We also toured the ancient city of Homer's Troy. It is just a rubble, but a thrill to stand on the very ground where Homer's

Ulysses once stood legendarily or victoriously. There is also hallowed ground on which I stood where the Hittites lived in Turkey. The Hittites, an ancient civilization, inhabited the land around 1300 BC, 3300 years ago, a perfect conclusion to a perfect tour.

Cappadocia, volcanic eruptions made into living quarters

After that glorious trip, I just toured by myself or with friends, Ireland, Scotland, Paris, Spain, England, Mexico, Argentina, China and Japan.

Ireland is a jolly place. I took my sons, Sean and Roark, with me on a bus tour. Roark deserted the bus, then Sean, then even I had to abandon the bus. I rented a car and we traveled the country and met up with the group each evening because our hotel rooms were prepaid. The car we leased was the only one the dealer had left so we had to take it. The floorboard was worn through and the moving road was visible as we merrily drove along on the left and hoped we remembered to stay in that ridiculous lane. The reason we left the bus was that it only stopped at places where we were hassled to buy Aran sweaters or Claddagh rings. All other places where we might have wanted to shop were closed for a myriad of reasons. Besides "shopping" was not the object of my taking my sons to the land of their heritage.

Only in Ireland

50
YEARS

The largest search for the mythical
Loch Ness monster in more than
50 years is underway at the Scottish
lake where purported sightings
of a massive creature of unknown
type or origin date back as far as the
sixth century A.D.

The Epoch Times, September 5, 2023

I took Roark with me on a trip to Scotland. In a small town, Inverness, famous for Loch Ness where a monster (the Loch Ness monster) supposedly resides. He did not show himself to us when we were there. Having no other points of interest our landlady suggested that we visit the graveyard. We duly went to the local graveyard. It was in a lovely wooded area with a winding path through the trees. At intervals one would come across a tombstone with a typical engraving as such: The McDougal Family or The

Fitzgerald Family with the individual names of the deceased below. After winding through the refreshing little forest the path led to a field of weeds. There in the stark sunlight lay a slab ten feet long and four feet wide flat in the ground. It is simply engraved: "The English are buried here."

Skara Brae

While in Scotland, I visited the Orkney Islands. I really wanted to go to the Shetland Islands to see the ponies, but the British had established a military base there. Tourists were not allowed. As a result, I settled for the Orkneys which was fortunate because they have something that aces the ponies, a Stone Age discovery. Skara Brae on Mainland Island of the Orkney Islands is a Stone Age settlement. The walls and the furniture were all carved of stone. A huge tidal wave had come over the island in 1850 and when it receded the Stone Age house was uncovered for people like me to marvel. Since then, due to another tidal wave and the labor of excavators, a whole village has been unearthed. It is unfortunate that "The Flintstones" is no longer a popular cartoon because Orkney would be a great place to take children to make Fred Flintstone and man's history come alive.

I took my daughter Kerry on a trip to Spain. We visited all the places pictured in my Spanish language textbook. While visiting the Alhambra, we met a local man and we asked him if he knew a good place to see flamenco. He said, "You do not *see* flamenco, you *do* flamenco." He recommended a cave where the Spanish people themselves go and it was a thrilling evening into night into dawn. The longer we stayed, the more dramatic the dancers. We were drained, but sated.

Not every experience was that positive. We went to a soccer game and, after it was over, the police had to rescue us and shepherd us to our car because the male soccer fans were crushing my blonde, blue-eyed daughter. The police were right on the spot so it seemed other American women must have naively come before us.

I rented a car, only a shift was available, of course. We were in a small town and riding around to look it over. I steered into a narrow winding road which led up a hill. I continued to the top and, upon reaching the summit, had a surprise, a shock really. The other side of the hill was just a staircase going down. There was no way out but to put down the clutch and shift into reverse and back down that narrow winding road and hope no one was in the way.

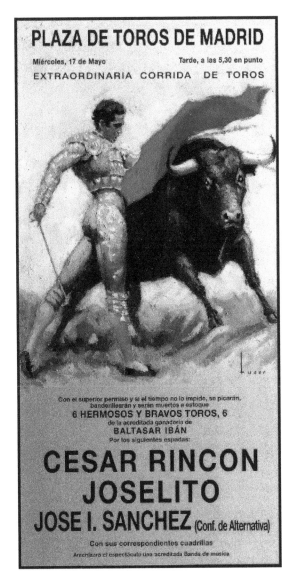

PLAZA DE TOROS DE MADRID

Miércoles, 17 de Mayo   Tarde, a las 5,30 en punto

EXTRAORDINARIA CORRIDA DE TOROS

Con el superior permiso y si el tiempo no lo impide, se picarán,
banderillearán y serán muertos a estoque
6 HERMOSOS Y BRAVOS TOROS, 6
de la acreditada ganadería de
BALTASAR IBÁN
Por los siguientes espadas:

CESAR RINCON
JOSELITO
JOSE I. SANCHEZ (Conf. de Alternativa)

Con sus correspondientes cuadrillas
Amenizará el espectáculo una acreditada Banda de música

Bullfighting was still popular in Spain when we were there so we went to check it out. It is a brutal sport. The toreador teases the bull to a state of anger because it is a bull-*fight*, then the matador thrusts his sword into the bull's vital spot. When the bull falls trumpets blare and a crew comes out and drags the poor animal away. A new bull is brought out for the second matador to show his skills and that bull is dragged from the arena, trumpets blaring and so forth, and that goes on for a whole afternoon.

I took Sean on a trip to Italy. We saw all the churches, monuments and fountains. On seeing Michelangelo's David, one tourist remarked, "Oh my, they would never allow that in Ireland." The best result of that trip was I met a family that became lifelong friends.

Nancy, my partner in a gay rooming house, and I took a trip to China and Japan. It was her idea. We were taken from the airport to our hotel by a young, attractive Chinese girl who spoke fluent English. We never saw her again but our trip was well organized. Sometimes we traveled alone and sometimes we met with other tourists. We were always under surveillance. The first thing we saw were old people sweeping the road with homemade brooms near a section with acres of hovels. Each unit was about the size of a Great Dane kennel, but better than living on the street. Instead of pedestrians in that section, everyone was on a bicycle made by the Wright brothers.

The hotel was elegant, right on Tiananmen Square. First trip, the zoo to see the pandas. It was very cold there in early spring. I bought a three-quarter length leopard coat for sixty dollars in one of the hotel's tony shops. American money went far in China. There were men on the streets whispering "Shange, shange." We thought that they were begging for coins. They were not and they were not begging. The poor

126

men were asking to exchange their little money for big money. In China, the workers were paid with bills about four inches long and two inches wide to distinguish their money from other people's money. The workers, thereby, were only allowed to purchase necessities, nothing luxurious. Most of the people were dressed alike, shapeless trousers and boxy, padded jackets buttoned to the neck, all in somber colors like gray or olive.

The people's little money

Rich people's money

Next, we were taken to the Great Wall. It is very, very great. After that, we were allowed to roam the city for a few days before we left for Shanghai, a city so crowded that you were at least sixth in line in any store. We were taken by hydrofoil to Macau, an island

and a world-famous gambling casino where no expense was spared for architecture, furnishings or landscaping. Neither Nancy nor I took any chances.

Next, we went to Hong Kong where we stayed for a couple of days. I do not remember why, but we took a cable car to the top of a mountain. We dined in a nice restaurant and ordered Peking duck. When I was young, the capital of China was Peking. I was told that it was always Beijing, but the Americans mispronounced it and changed it to Peking and the Chinese were restoring the city's real name. The duck, however, stuck to the misnomer. Hong Kong is a large, modern city with skyscrapers like New York. One noticeable difference is that in Hong Kong laundry is hanging out to dry everywhere even on the terraces of luxury buildings. We visited Taiwan. Everyone there travels on a Vesper or a motor scooter of some kind. Whole families ride on one vehicle, hanging on for dear life as it zips along, arms, legs and shopping bags flying in the wind.

We flew to Tokyo, Japan, a city that bespeaks its country's wealth with restaurants and food shops everywhere and coffee machines on every other corner. The women were in colorful silks and the men in business suits. There were few autos because the tax to own one was the same cost as the price of the car. A rule that deterred the populous from cluttering up that small island nation. To compensate, the government built a comprehensive subway system for the people. It terrified me, so I did not do much exploring in Tokyo.

We did though, take the bullet train to Kyoto, a city renowned for its gardens. In Kyoto, every window is a picture frame. When the viewer peers out, he beholds a scene arranged like a tableau with trees, grass and flowers and perhaps a graceful teahouse or cottage. Kyoto was a perfect ending to our far eastern trip, but it made it that much more difficult to get used to the soot, and dust, and smoke, and rust.

In March 2002, I took a trip to Cuba with my daughter Tracey. Americans were not allowed to travel to Cuba because of political reasons, but certain church groups and educational trips were permitted. Alumni from Mount Holyoke, Tracey's alma mater, were partnering with Harvard alumni to tour Cuba for educational purposes. It was evident while we were there why Castro did not want Americans to see how poorly Cubans were fairing under his restrictive form of government. No one was permitted to make a living on his own initiative. No one could have a business unless he were on a list; tailor, barber, etc. Restaurants were only allowed if all the employees were family members and guests were served in the restaurateur's home. Certain artists and artisans were permitted to vend their self-made wares near the old fort in Havana. That was the extent of capitalism.

Tracey was enterprising. She bought tickets for a baseball game where it was nice to see the fans smiling and happy which was rare in that somber land. However, we missed all the wisecracks and funny remarks in the bleachers that go with a ballgame because neither of us understood Spanish.

Tracey also surprised me with tickets to the ballet, established and directed by Alicia Alonzo who, in America, was famous to dance patrons. It was lovely and beautiful. In Lincoln Center in New York, where ballets are performed, the audiences are usually filled with ladies young and old, but in Cuba, the theatre was filled with young men and women couples in their twenties and thirties.

Four inch hand-carved rocker made of horn by a Cuban artisan/vender

We went to Guantanamo Bay, but were only allowed to see the prison from a bluff above where they provided a "pay to look" kind of telescope.

In Havana, many walls were graffitied with revolutionary slogans. Che Guevara's portrait was on display everywhere and there was a big billboard-type tribute to Ethel and Julius Rosenberg, American spies from World War II, who were executed in the electric chair.

Monument to the Rosenbergs

Havana has a plain, but very nice, art museum. It is filled with extraordinary works by local artists, people expressing their sorrow from the soul for their isolation. Visiting Cuba was an emotional experience never to be forgotten.

One of the first books I read on my Kindle was taken from the diary of Charles Darwin that he kept on his around-the-world journey aboard the HMS Beagle. Darwin was 22 years old, a geologist, naturalist and biologist. It was his task to draw maps of the coastline of South America with its geological formations as well as its coastline and its indentations. He also recorded the appearances and habits of the birds and animals.

When he reached the southern tip of the continent, he recorded his impression of the native people, the Yahgan and Ona tribes in Tierra del Fuego (Land of Fire). That name was given to that place so near the South Pole because sailors had observed many bonfires on the land as they sailed by. The reason for the bonfires was that it was cold and the natives had no clothes and no shelter. They built fires to keep warm even in their canoes. They had no cloth fabric and no knowledge of weaving or sewing. Darwin remarked on how backward these natives were and described their language as sounding like grunts.

Darwin's description made me want to visit the end of the earth. I flew to Buenos Aires and took a smaller plane to Ushuaia, Tierra del Fuego's little city lying in a small nest of mountains where a standard airline could neither land nor take off. Ushuaia is sparsely settled and is a "free" city. No one collects import or export taxes there. Whiskey is cheap.

In the 1860s, George Despard, a British minister, started a mission and raised his family in Tierra del Fuego. He and his sons taught the natives carpentry and how to build houses, how to raise sheep and how to plant gardens for food. The sons and their father learned the language of the natives and it made the savages more friendly. After many years of serving his mission, Despard's compound was raided by the natives. The minister returned to England after living for years and raising his family at the tip of South America. His oldest son, an adopted child, Thomas Bridges, chose to stay and raise sheep. The Argentinean government granted him a large tract of land for his services to the country. Bridges, in his later years, moved to England and compiled a dictionary of the Yahgan and Ona languages. After 7,000 years the tribes are now extinct.

A "house" in Tierra del Fuego

Stone Age statues found in Malta depict bulbous women

One of my last adventures, and one of the best, was when Tracey and I took a trip to Sicily. She is a marvelous trip planner. We planned to visit Malta while over there. To my surprise, my smart daughter had made plans for us to be admitted to a special place where pre-arrangement for admittance was necessary. She did this on the computer before we left home.

Malta is composed of three islands; the main one, a small uninhabited one and a third, sparsely inhabited and containing the special place to which we would be admitted. It was a stone-age site unearthed and preserved by the Maltese. It resembled the Orkney Island site but had stone doors in addition to the stone walls and furniture.

Malta has many other unusual historic places. A co-cathedral, St. John's, contains elaborate side altars where Crusaders' remains are encrypted. The shrines were pre-commissioned by the Crusaders themselves, each langue (division) trying to outdo the other with its own memorial. Malta was the scene of many battles in ancient times. The fort and solid ramparts are still there.

A Basilica outside of the city dedicated to Mary has a rotunda with stained glass windows all around and the world's third-largest, unsupported glass dome. What makes it a tourist attraction is that a large German bomb pierced its glass dome, fell to the floor while Mass was in progress and failed to explode. It was a miracle.

Rotunda of Sanctuary Basilica, Malta

A ferry runs from Malta to the tip of Sicily. Since Tracey was a Classics major in college, she was a great tourist guide for me. Her enthusiasm for this part of the world was like mine when standing on the site of the Hittites. She had studied about the battles between ancient peoples here, their successes and defeats. She had read of the early settlements there of Phoenicians, from Carthage and elsewhere, and the Ancient Greeks and Romans who settled on the Island.

We rented a car and toured the island of Sicily to exhaustion. We also had a local guide who told stories about each of the ruins of Greek-styled temples strewn over the landscape. The island was a hot spot in the time of the Punic Wars and true history is mingled with myth and legend.

A very special place we visited was the Villa Romana del Casale now famous for its spectacular mosaics. The favorite room is the girls' gymnasium that features ten girls in bikinis posed in athletic positions. All the rooms in the Villa overflow with mosaics but the girls, like the Sixteen Dancing Darlings, take the cake. We were fortunate that workmen were still unearthing the treasure when we arrived and the government had not yet clamped its paws on the freedom of exploration. On a later trip to Sicily and the Villa, we found tourists were only allowed to see the plumbing on the outside.

Mosaic of women athletes at the Villa Romana del Casale

In 2004, my daughters, Tracey and Kerry, and my daughter-in-law Mary and I, went to a Mexican spa. We were pampered with facials, massages and good Mexican food. The spa was near Taxco, a town that sits on a mountain of silver. Every shop is owned by a silversmith and their wares are unusual, irresistible and inexpensive. On the way back to Mexico City, we stopped at the house of Frida Kahlo-that audacious Mexican artist. She had a tumultuous marriage to the muralist Diego Rivera. Their houses were connected on the 2nd floor with a passageway traversing about 20 feet. We had a little time for sightseeing in Mexico City where stands the poignant monument called "Monumento a los Niños Héroes" dedicated to young Mexican soldiers, combatants against the United States invasion in 1846.

Besides all these wonderful exotic places, I traveled on the home continent as well. Victoria, a small city over the border in Canada, has flowers everywhere reminiscent of London. The streets are red brick, quaint and picturesque, but the sidewalks, when I was there, were cluttered with "lost" young men and women lying each on a blanket, usually with a dog, with a handout for charity. The permanent residents, working people, were annoyed at these youths coming into the city from the hinterlands and spoiling their "pretty city" environment.

Montreal is remembered for its frigid temperature and its compensation by building a whole city underground so fragile visitors do not have to walk in the snowy streets.

Victoria, Canada

California has great weather.

The Southwest has an allure like no other part of our nation. One reason being its breathtaking landscapes and its large congregation of frontier artists. In addition to painters, there are many metal smiths and stonecutters who work with silver and turquoise, natural resources found in the southwestern states. For those who study Native Americans' history, there are the cave-dwellers, relocated tribes and archaeological sites, all plentiful.

Texas has scenic Corpus Christi on the Gulf of Mexico; San Antonio, a living history book of a town; and Austin, the capital and a modern, vibrant city popular for being the live music capital of the world.

The Grand Canyon, Bryce Canyon and Yellowstone are perfect if you like the outdoors. Atlanta, Georgia has restaurants that make your palette sing, and if you like the beach, head to Florida.

Those are all places I visited here in my home country.

In England, I toured the Roman baths, Jane Austin's house, the home of Isaac Newton and the white cliffs of Dover.

In France, besides Paris, I toured Cannes during the film festival, Omaha Beach and La Côte d'Azur.

In Ireland, coast to coast, top to bottom, twice.

Other places I went on short tourist trips were Austria-Hungary, Czechoslovakia, Greece, Mexico, Rio de Janeiro and Barcelona.

My favorite place? Egypt.

27

Movin' on Up

When my grandfather Gaitings died, I inherited a small sum of money. I put it down on a tired old house in a tired old neighborhood in Woodside, Queens. My first tenants were a nice Hispanic family. A neighbor who planted herself on her front stoop every day called me over to say, "Why you renta to doze people? They dona even spika da English."

I refurbished the basement of the old house and made an illegal studio apartment to rent. My first tenant there was a young man with a dog. He stayed a couple of months and then left, leaving his dog in lieu of rent. I think it was a dog. It weighed more than I.

Off to a kennel he went and, of course, I had to pay his room and board. After a week and a big bill, I begged the kennel keeper to take the dog and sell him. He did. I put the old house up for sale and realtors started showing it.

Around that time, I happened to be up very early one morning and was washing the windows in the front room of my apartment. While standing on the radiator cover and window sill to clean the top outside pane, I had a perfect view of the street below and my MG parked there. A man came along carrying a long object with which he started to smash the windshield of my precious little roadster. I recognized the smasher at that moment as being the tenant from the tired old house — the nice Hispanic family man, not the old English sheep dog deserter.

I dressed and walked to the local precinct and reported the vandalism to my car. I was brushed off and, literally, thrown out of the police station with the remark that I had no evidence. This is why people buy guns.

In 1983, I bought a 200-year-old house in a rather run-down section of downtown Brooklyn called Boerum Hill. The area has since revived and is in great demand today.

When I went to research the property at the Brooklyn Historical Society, they actually handed me papers handwritten at the time King George was granting land. I was afraid to touch them and wondered at the naivety of the Historical volunteer.

My 200-year-old Brooklyn house. The gap on the left is two feet wider at the bottom.

The house leans two feet to the left and pedestrians often stop and point. Water was coming from everywhere; the roof, the radiators, the basement.

I just had to camp out there for a while until everything was fixed. The house was a two- family and my first tenant was Lincoln Paine, as in Thomas Paine, the patriot, of whom he was a descendant. He had just graduated from Columbia.

"What was your major?"

"Latin."

"The apartment is yours."

After Lincoln settled in, he started a corporation. I asked, "What does your corporation do?" He said, "We gather the tall ships for centennials."

After a few years, Lincoln met a girl and married. He moved to a larger apartment in another building and left me with his cat, Alice — because his wife's name was Alice.

Speaking of cats, one morning I awoke to a racket. Two cats were duking it out on my sunroom roof right outside my bedroom window, a ring-side seat. There was a lot of noise, hissing and caterwauling before they collided. The cats formed a big fur ball with eight paws like a spiked mace waving and battering. The fur ball started to roll, one cat on top and then the other with all paws waving about. They were two man-eating tigers trying to kill each other. The ball continued to roll slowly. To my horror, it rolled right off the roof onto the flagstones below. I thought cats were smarter than that. They were gone by the time I went to the yard. They had to climb a six-foot anchor fence to leave. So, it's true, cats do have nine lives.

The neighborhood was near enough to Brooklyn Technical High School where I was teaching English, so I could walk to work. After a few years, I retired from teaching because I was losing my hearing.

I had a student in Brooklyn Technical High School whom I liked very much. She was from Puerto Rico and a straight "A" student. She sat in the front row in the seat nearest to my desk so she would not miss a word of the lesson. The class was right after the lunch period. One day, she entered the classroom, sat down and put her head on the desk. I asked if she was all right and if there was anything I could do. Her classmate friends assured me that she was all right — just not feeling well. My "A" student started to weep silently. The tears were drowning the desk. She continued to weep, then sob and the tears were beginning to roll off the desk onto the floor. Soon there was a small river of tears running alongside my desk.

As soon as the period ended, I took "A" to the infirmary where she started to hallucinate. She said repeatedly through tears, "Dr. Malloy, don't leave me." (After I earned my Juris Doctorate, she always addressed me as "Doctor.") The nurse took charge until her dad came to bring her home. Now what was that about? Some troublesome students had laced my "A" student's drink in the lunchroom with narcotics. Jealousy is the worst of the Seven Deadly Sins. The whole event was hushed up and swept under the rug and no one was punished.

The sequel to this tale is that the "A" student graduated, took a job in the Midwest, went to law school, and now sits on the highest bench, the Appellate Court of that Midwestern state — the first Puerto Rican woman to have achieved that distinction. I am so proud of her. The girl who addressed me as "Doctor" is now herself addressed as "The

Honorable."

In MCMLXXIX (1979), I opened a law office in my house, which was well-suited for that because it had a separate entrance to the lower floor from the street. I practiced there for 20 years.

As I write this, it is the year 2023. Every evening on television a bright young salesman tells the audience that their homes are in jeopardy of being stolen if they do not have title insurance. That may seem ridiculous in most parts of the United States but in Brooklyn, house stealing is a common occurrence.

When I was practicing real estate law in Brooklyn, I heard of several such instances and had it happen to two of my own clients. First, there was Mrs. B, a 90-year-old woman who lived alone. A friendly neighbor who lived across the street and was known to Mrs. B, offered to help her fill out papers to obtain a mortgage. He gave her papers to sign, a Deed being among them, and stole her house. When he claimed possession, Mrs. B's grown children took her to the office of the district attorney. He tried to shoo the family from his office saying it was not within the purview of his department. That did not work and the B family held fast and, when they threatened to go to the press, the district attorney conceded and Mrs. B was eventually given back her house. The "good neighbor" was never punished.

The second building theft consisted of a three-story building with a store and two apartments above. One day, when the Reverend X came to collect the rent, he was locked out. He proceeded to break in when the "new owner" appeared and threatened him with physical harm if he did not leave. He called me. I took a copy of the Reverend's Deed from my file and went across the street to the firehouse and asked the firemen to help. They jumped in their hook and ladder and drove it just around the corner and confronted the "new owner" with a copy of the Deed. The thief then produced a copy of his Deed. The firemen showed it to me. I saw that it was notarized by an attorney who was an acquaintance. I called him. He said, "Wow, my notary stamp was stolen a month ago and I reported it to the police." The firemen dislodged the "new owner" and the old Reverend was given back possession. The building thief was never punished for that crime.

The third building theft was recounted to me by a fellow attorney. His client was on an extended trip. When she returned home, she found it occupied by a stranger who had broken in and taken possession. The woman notified her lawyer and the authorities and was able to regain possession. However, the thief had sold some of her things including her baby grand piano.

One day, a prospective client walked into my law office with a problem involving her father's estate in Puerto Rico. It was not my area of law practice nor was it in my jurisdiction. However, it turned out that the erstwhile client was a jeweler, a person who actually made fine gold and silver pieces from raw metal to a finished jewel. I was very interested. The result of this meeting was, I started a factory to make fine Irish jewelry. My daughter, Kerry presented me with a priceless gift; the domain "irishjewelry.com."

Marly
Malone

My jeweler and her partner, I'll call them Mona and Lucy, produced hundreds of precious pieces that I marketed in an Irish store in Rockefeller Center and on the internet. My mother had left me many samples of antique jewelry, brooches, pendants, rings, etc. Mona ordered rubber molds made of each piece, one thousand molds in six years. The process went something like this as I remember it: molten wax was poured into a mold of a ring, let's say, with a stem attached. When the wax hardened, it was removed from the mold and attached to a "tree" by its stem with other wax pieces. When the "tree" was full, it was put in a cylinder and liquid plaster filled the cylinder and, when the plaster hardened, it was placed in a special high-degree oven. The wax would go up in smoke leaving a void in the shape of the little tree of jewels. Molten gold or silver was poured into the spaces vacated by the evaporated wax. When the precious metal "tree" cooled the "branches," the pieces, were cut off, trimmed and made ready for polishing and soldering of clasps, pins, hinges or whatever was needed. Besides casting, Mona made rosaries and necklaces from semi-precious stones such as garnet, amethyst, topaz or cultured pearls and sterling silver wire.

After six years, Mona and Lucy disengaged, so I closed the factory and sold the domain name. Mona bought the jewelry making equipment from me, so I'm sure she has her own factory somewhere. Before she left, Lucy told me that Mona had been filching small amounts of gold all along, which of course I already knew. Where else could all those gold stems from the tree have gone? Lucy returned to Puerto Rico and became a police officer.

During my time as an attorney, I bought some other properties to rent out. One was a rooming house occupied by gay men. They were bad boys and gave me a headache. By that, I mean that they deliberately destroyed the building by breaking the balustrade, pulling doors off hinges and letting water overflow the sinks, onto the floor and down the stairs. They compounded this by making complaints to the building department authorities causing summonses and fines being issued. They also robbed one another.

One early Sunday morning, I went to the building to check the trash and sweep the sidewalk. There was a fenced-in vacant lot next to the house and a young girl appeared in the lot. She asked if she could use my stoop to climb out and, of course, I said, "Yes." After the rescue of the young "professional," I took the liberty to say, "Why do you work at this hard job?" She replied, "Oh, it ain't hard" — end of conversation.

Another tenant I shall call Dotty Deadbeat for the sake of privacy, never paid the rent so I had to evict her. Now, 40 years later, she crosses my path. Dotty is now a professional impersonator of Tina Turner and appears on stage in Las Vegas. I know this because my son, a musician with a band, has the same agent as Dotty and he recognized and remembered her from those hard Brooklyn days.

A favorite tenant of mine sat on a second story window sill and, forgetting that the window was open, leaned back and fell 20 feet into a slate pit and after being patched up in a hospital, lived to tell it. He and a roommate moved into my carriage house. After not paying the rent for three months, I wrote them a letter explaining why I needed to get paid. The pair appeared at my door. I admitted them and we sat down around a small table. Without preliminary, the girl said, "We're heroin addicts." Shocked to the socks, I said, "I'm sorry to hear that."

The story has a happy ending. They paid up and cleaned up themselves. She became a teacher and he became a successful criminal lawyer. He was so good at his profession, and still is, because he believes that all his clients are innocent.

In 1983, my car was a two-seater Roadster MG (Morris Garage). A very impractical vehicle for the city, especially raw Brooklyn. I wanted to move from Queens to Brooklyn to be near my job, but I had to have a place with a garage to keep my little car safe from vandals. One day, like a gift from God, I saw an ad in the New York Times offering for sale a package of two buildings facing a corner with a carriage house. They were "shells" meaning "not livable condition" and the price was affordable - $35,000. I sold my apartment in Queens and, with a partner, a real estate broker whom I was dating, bought the package of shells. My partner was only interested in "flipping" real estate, but I wanted to renovate. He acquiesced, but did not contribute funds other than half the purchase price.

The corner building had a large yellow symbol prominently painted on the front and one foot square with an X in the middle. It stands for "unsafe building," painted there by the fire department to warn firemen about entering. The building had a burned-out roof and staircase from a previous fire. Further, it bulged out three feet on the east side. It was so hazardous that I had to go to court and get legal permission to renovate. That entailed hiring an architect and an engineer. Metal piles had to be driven into the ground and tall enough to hold floors

(Before) Being stabilized

one, two, three and four. It needed a new roof and stairs from bottom to top, new windows and floors throughout with frequent Department of Buildings inspections at every step.

After the inside was stabilized, the huge bulge on the outside had to be addressed. That was cosmetically solved by filling in the low spots with cement and finishing the brownstone with a whole new coat. One of the results was exceptionally wide window sills on the inside.

(After) The art of brownstoning

Brownstone is made by using cement with brown coloring added, applied smoothly to an exterior and then horizontal and perpendicular grooves are deeply indented to make the appearance of a house being built of huge blocks of stone about two feet wide and one foot high. It takes an experienced mason to do brown-stoning. Pakistani immigrants, of which there are many in Brooklyn, are particularly adept at this dying tradition and their skills are in great demand.

Sometime in the history of that old corner building, someone had lowered the traditional parlor floor to ground level to make a grocery store. This created problems for making efficient and attractive layouts of the space. Eventually, the problem was solved by creating a new entrance door at street level for the bottom apartment and the top apartment used the original entrance up a stoop.

The townhouse eventually became livable, but not luxurious and I started to collect rent. My "partner" sued me for "specific performance" which means I must sell and pay him his half. My attorney worked out a deal and I paid off the partner with $100,000.

A second building next to the corner was also in bad shape. It had no heat, hot water or gas. The flooring on the parlor floor was seven inches higher on one end than the other. The whole thing had to be replaced and beams on one end shaved and on the other end built up. The back wall of the building on the second floor was sixteen inches from the bedroom floor so you could look down into the yard from up there. The entire four-story brick wall had to come down and rebuilt brick by brick.

The bathroom fixtures had all been smashed to pieces by vandals and all the cabinet doors wrenched from their hinges. It took a while to make it livable, but I continued to upgrade for 30 years.

Every apartment had a dishwasher, a washing machine, a dryer, new windows, new floors, new bathrooms and kitchens. Each apartment had its own heating system and hot water and every apartment had a working, open fireplace.

Last to be renovated was the jewel of the "package," the carriage house, which had been the reason for my purchase in the first place to protect my MG from vandals. Well before that happened, the little Roadster caught fire one night while parked on the street and that was the end of my owning an impractical auto.

The carriage house

The carriage house had one large room with a dirt floor for the horse and carriage and a stair to a loft with a fireplace and a bathroom for the coachman. First, a floor was installed and the large room was divided into a kitchen and sitting room. The back wall was opened and a French door was installed opening to a terrace and garden. Upstairs became one large bedroom, one small bedroom and a new bath. I installed new front windows accented with stained glass.

Everyone wanted to live in the carriage house. There was a space, a driveway between the corner building and the carriage house where I kept my Mercedes forevermore. It had one of the most precious features of all things in downtown Brooklyn, a legal curb cut.

In 2020, now a permanent Florida resident, I was offered six million dollars for "the package." I took it.

28

Breukelen

Other than my baby years, before my family became pioneers in Queens, I spent 36 years as an adult, one-third of my life, living in Brooklyn, a marvelous place and a world of its own from the East River to the Atlantic Ocean.

I now take you on a tour of this wondrous place. Three-quarters of the perimeter is waterfront and it has canals as well. Gowanus Canal near my house was built for commerce where ships could pick up manufactured goods from the many small factories in the borough. Now, it is desired waterfront property bordered by expensive condominiums.

The borough of Queens is laid out on a grid. For example, the avenues are numbered and run east to west while streets, also numbered, run north to south. Building addresses are determined by the nearest intersection of a street and avenue. Brooklyn is a bowl of spaghetti. The old streets curve in all directions, many times depending upon where the Native Americans made their trails. Instead of numbers, the streets are named for the original Dutch settlers such as Schermerhorn Street. The puzzle is challenging and makes life interesting.

The northwest coast of Brooklyn is married to Manhattan by the Williamsburg, Manhattan and Brooklyn Bridges and the Brooklyn Battery Tunnel. The south borders the Atlantic Ocean and has Coney Island, a famous resort and playground with groundbreaking roller coaster rides for thrills, a beach and a boardwalk with the usual tacky booths. Next to Coney is Brighten Beach where Russian immigrants have settled. It is fondly referred to as "Little Odessa" and is notorious for its Russian and Ukrainian gangsters. Further north on the coast is Sheepshead Bay where Ursula and I would have lunch in one of the seafood restaurants and wait for the boats to come in so we could buy fresh fish from the fishermen in the marina. There is always a Japanese restaurant person waiting on the shore in case a captain brings in an eel.

Brooklyn, as well as being its own city, had its own diocese, cathedral and Monsignor as well. It is St. James Cathedral, located on Jay Street and within walking distance of my house. One Sunday morning as I was taking a shortcut across the Metrotech campus, I saw a dog, all alone. There was no one around at that hour of the day. As I approached the animal, I noticed he was a service dog with a harness and square handle. I wanted to notify the ASPCA or the police, but I did not have my flip phone with me. He remained still so I went nearer. Then I discovered the joke was on me. He was a newly installed statue. Fortunately, no one was about to see my embarrassment.

I arrived at church and took my seat. The first two pews were reserved for the deaf and they had a signer for the sermon. As I sat there contemplating, I decided I should learn Sign Language because I was getting more deaf as the years went by. After Mass, I went to the sacristy to speak to Marie. The sacristy is a room off the main altar where the priest and altar boys don their cassocks and vestments for Mass. Marie is the signer for the deaf. I asked her if she would give me lessons to learn Sign Language.

She seemed a bit horrified and said, "No, no, no, I could not."

"Why? I'll pay you and I can come to you if you can't come to my place."

"No, no, no, I couldn't — Monsignor…"

"It's alright Marie, I will find someone else to give me lessons."

"Lessons! I thought you said blessings!"

We both laughed. She really was hard of hearing. Two hard-of-hearing people trying to converse is a comedy routine.

Brooklyn is also known as "The Borough of Churches." There is a church or two on every other block, many of them cathedrals. Every ethnic group has its own neighborhood and its own church where sermons are delivered in the language of their native country. Most of these churches have been rescued from the dust heap and renovated by the new populations for their own denomination. Brooklyn has a section for almost every nationality in the world from the Caribbean, Africa, Europe and Asia. All bring their special skills and exotic foods to enrich the borough.

159

The Chinese have a small Chinatown even though there is the famous Chinatown of books and films right across the river in Manhattan. The Arabs settled on and around Atlantic Avenue from the East River toward the interior with Christians on the west end and Muslims on the east. There are Jewish communities such as Williamsburg and Borough Park sprinkled all over Brooklyn with different degrees of Orthodoxy and Reform. There are groups from Bangladesh, Puerto Rico, Haiti, Pakistan and many other places and grocery stores that cater to each of their particular tastes. Brooklyn is the true melting pot with very rich, very poor and in between.

Prospect Park is the heart of Brooklyn. Its main entrance is in front of the Sailor's and Soldier's Monument, a giant arch set in a circle from which radiate the main highways running like spokes to the outer reaches of the county, Flatbush Avenue, Eastern Parkway, Ocean Parkway. The Arch is momentous, like the Arc de Triomphe. It was built in 1889 and dedicated to the men who fought in the Civil War. That would include my great grandfather, Daniel Gaitings, who joined the Union forces at the age of seventeen.

Next to Prospect Park is the Brooklyn Botanical Garden where Ursula and I spent many idyllic hours among the flowers. It is famous for its lake and Japanese pagoda surrounded by blossoming cherry trees in the spring. Profuse beds of tulips in brilliant colors border the walkways. There is an herb garden, a field of rose arbors and a solarium with tropical plants. Prospect Park, built in 1865, is 526 acres of rolling hills. A circulating water system makes possible streams, little waterfalls and picturesque bridges. The park also has a bridle path. One part was left as a rugged wooded area and has woodland plants among the trees.

Brooklyn Soldiers' and Sailors' Arch

The main branch of the Brooklyn Public Library faces the Soldiers' and Sailors' Monument from the East. As a landmark, I would not recommend it as an example for its architecture. The groundbreaking was in 1912, but work did not begin until 1938 because it was over-priced and under-funded. As a result, although presently in use, the library has never been completed on the inside. The façade is Art Deco design, greatly admired in its era, but a startling contrast to the surrounding buildings built at the turn of the century or before. The one tasteful touch that improves the

161

scene is that the front entrance is accessed by a raised terrace with an imposing staircase leading up to the main door. One fact that the benefactors never fail to point out is that the building, from the air, appears to be a big open book. The only way anyone can see that book is if they take flight in a balloon.

Brooklyn Public Library

Next to the library rises the imposing Brooklyn Art Museum that faces Eastern Parkway. The museum houses a fine collection of ancient Egyptian artifacts. Other than that, its permanent collection is lean. Every few months, the museum will showcase a special artist and occasionally the exhibit will be noteworthy. Such was the showing of Nigerian artist El Anatsui who uses discarded detritus as a medium, such as beer cans, cigarette wrappers and, most of all, bottle caps. From these aluminum discards, Anatsui creates fluid wall hangings of breathtaking beauty. I wish everyone could see this artist's work with their own eyes. It is miraculous.

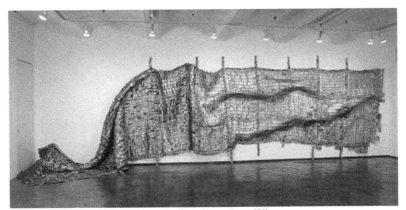

Anatsui, "Fading Scroll"

Anatsui, "Rain Has No Father"

The Brooklyn Museum is a worthy compliment to the grand Eastern Parkway, the first parkway ever to be built. Its creators were Frederick Law Olmstead and Calvert Vaux. Olmstead described it as "A shaded green ribbon." The parkway was built in 1870 and took over 63 acres of land. It is six lanes divided by a thirty-foot median plus a service road bordered by a footpath and bicycle run. The medians are planted with over one thousand trees, have benches and a sidewalk of asphalt tiles. Eastern Parkway was the first parkway ever to be conceived because it was built for recreation and private cars, commercial traffic being restricted. On September 26, 1983, Eastern Parkway was listed on the National Register of Historic Places.

The oldest building in Brooklyn is said to be the Wyckoff House built in 1652. It is a small wooden house that has been preserved and is open to the public as a museum. A rival antiquity is the Flatbush Reform Dutch Church. The parish was established in 1654. The present building is the third structure to be built on the site to replace the decaying earlier churches. Reconstruction has been necessary to keep the church standing.

Fort Greene is a part of Brooklyn inhabited by "pioneers," people who took the chance, bought a rundown house in a rundown section and worked to bring the neighborhood back to its former grandeur. The row townhouses and brownstones are larger than in other sections, and the area is bound on the west by Fort Greene Park. The park has a tumultuous history.

In the six years between 1776 and 1782, 11,500 soldier and sailor prisoners died on twelve British prison ships anchored in what is now Brooklyn Navy

Yard. The conditions were so unsanitary that all died of illness and disease caused by the overcrowding and neglect. For example, the ship *Jersey*, the most notorious, was built for 400 but was packed with 1,400 prisoners.

The patriots were given a choice by the Crown to join the British Army or perish. Few of the brave settlers took the king's offer and almost all remained true to their new country and their general, George Washington. King George had the prisoners designated "traitors" so they would not have prisoner-of-war status. Bodies of the dead were thrown overboard and eventually washed up on shore where bones and skulls remained until Brooklynites, by dredging and digging, collected as many remains as they could. In 1808, the bones were encrypted and buried in Fort Greene Park.

The people of Brooklyn had a planned vault and monument to honor those brave soldiers and sailors who were imprisoned. Funds were collected, but the corrupt politicians in Tammany Hall stole the money. Not until one hundred years later, in 1908, were a monument and a plaque dedicated and placed over the crypt containing the remains of those Revolutionary soldiers and sailors. The monument was designed by Stanford White. It is 149 feet tall with an eight-ton bronze beacon on top, resembling a lighthouse. It is called "The Prison Ship Martyrs' Monument."

After World War II, Fort Greene descended into slum status and the park along with the Prison Ship Monument were vandalized and desecrated severely. In 1960, a new plaque was dedicated on the monument and stands today. Fort Greene has become a neighborhood of young professionals.

The Prison Ship Martyrs' Monument

Other than the structures and landscaping in the heart of the borough, Brooklyn has many other interesting buildings and places. There is the Brooklyn Academy of Music where visiting theatrical companies, not needing a permanent venue, are featured such as Shen Yun from China, or the National Ballet from Ukraine. Between such bookings, it is used for art films.

Brooklyn City Hall, rendered by artist Lily Francis

In its early history, Brooklyn was a city in its own right. One of the last vestiges of those days is the Brooklyn Borough Hall which was originally Brooklyn City Hall. It was constructed of marble and built in 1848 in the style of a Greek temple. Fifty years later Brooklyn merged with New York City and became its poor little Cinderella stepsister even though it is far more beautiful, historical and interesting than Manhattan.

Near the northwest corner of Brooklyn, is a sparsely populated place with water all around. It does not have much to offer except a superb view of the Statue of Liberty and a fabulous place called 'The Lobster Pound' where lobster lovers may pick out their crustacean while it is swimming around in one of two huge tanks. Red Hook is aptly named and, when you see it on a map, it is a startling land formation. It is the only place in New York City from which you can see a view of the whole front of the Statue of Liberty and therefore is a favorite spot of photographers. See if you can find it on the map.

On the southern coast of Brooklyn, named Bay Ridge, is where the Verrazano Bridge to Staten Island had its moment of fame when it was built because it was the longest suspension bridge in the world, 13,700 feet. It has since been surpassed in length by bridges in China. If you live on Staten Island and work in Manhattan it costs $34 a day in tolls.

At Christmas time, Brooklyn puts on a fantastic "light" show in a section called Dyker Heights. The houses are luxurious and every homeowner has created a fabulous scene, each one outdoing the other. Lawns are decorated with reindeer, dwarfs, Christmas trees, etc. all covered with lights as well. It is difficult to describe the effect of thousands and thousands of little light bulbs lighting up a whole neighborhood. The undertaking of the people in Dyker Heights is astounding. Their effort has become so famous that three-and-a-half hour tours are run from Union Square in Manhattan during the season but you can get a free virtual tour of this extraordinary holiday event in Brooklyn on the internet.

Running south on Third Avenue in Sunset Park, Brooklyn takes on a somber atmosphere. The street is dark due to the overhead section of the Brooklyn Queens Expressway, commonly called the BQE. It is strictly a commercial area, a large part of which is set aside for small manufacturers and artisans such as metal workers and stained-glass artisans. They are housed in medium high-rise buildings. The area is an Industrial Park. In the midst of this outdoor dungeon between Upper New York Bay and Third Avenue, looms the notorious MDC (Metropolitan Detention Center). It is known for its brutality to both inmates and guards. Two of its infamous inmates of the moment are Ghislaine Maxwell and rapper Robert Kelly.

The Brooklyn Bridge is one of the most famous bridges in the world due to its unusual design and beauty and, strangely, to a man who died in jail. Building began in 1869 and took sixteen years to complete. Its architect was John A. Roebling who gave his life in the building of the bridge when he suffered decompression sickness after descending with the workmen into one of the deep piles necessary for a suspension bridge. After his death, his son and daughter-in-law carried on the work, but both succumbed before the bridge was completed.

Remembrance of the Twin Towers

The Brooklyn Bridge is famous for its antebellum design, particularly for the Gothic cathedral arches that distinguish it from any other bridge. They rise 100 feet and are made of limestone, granite and cement. On the day of its opening in 1883, there was a big celebration attended by notable politicians including the President of the United States Chester A. Arthur. At that time, it cost ten cents for a horse and wagon to cross the bridge.

The opening of the Brooklyn Bridge, May 24, 1883.
President Chester A. Arthur and his party cross the bridge.

In 1983, I had the good fortune to attend a party in honor of the Brooklyn Bridge's 100th birthday. It was fortuitous that that particular evening I ran into an old friend who had a college roommate who was having the party and did not mind if I joined in. How lucky I was that night. The party was held in an apartment high up overlooking the East River very close to the bridge. The expansive windows gave all the guests plenty of room to watch the fireworks. We were so close to the conflagration that we instinctively ducked when we heard the initial crack before each explosion of light. After half an hour, my jaws ached from the constant smiling of delight. The celebration ended when a huge blanket of stars unfurled from the walkway of the bridge down to the river. It was unforgettable.

On March 16, 1816, an unheralded genius by the name of George C. Parker was born. You will not recognize his name, but you have heard of his deeds. Mr. Parker is the man who sold the Brooklyn Bridge to gullible immigrants. It is said that he sold the bridge twice a week for many years. Parker set up a fake office and presented forged documents to convince his victims of his legitimacy. The police would have to stop the victims when they attempted to set up toll booths on the bridge. Parker also tried to sell the Statue of Liberty and the Metropolitan Museum of Art. When touting Grant's Tomb, he pretended to be Grant's grandson.

Parker was arrested four times and finally sent to Sing for life. Instead of saving this fellow's genius for something useful like selling defective armaments to our enemies, they let it rust away in jail. Believe that and I have a bridge to sell you.

29

Vend-etta

My mother was a collector, so I, her only heir, inherited a large treasure of antiques. In my sunset years, my inheritance was getting claustrophobic so I started a new career, I became a vender.

I joined a really great group of people who sold their wares every weekend in the schoolyard on 7th Avenue in Park Slope. Every Saturday and Sunday I would rise at 5 A.M. and be on site by 6 A.M. in order to secure a parking space in front of the school. I set up my booth under a slide and some parallel bars which enabled me to spread an awning to block the sun.

It was not the money that drove me to pack and haul heavy boxes, set up tables and stand all day, it was the legacy that prevented me from throwing away 100-year-old porcelain figurines, toys, dolls, laces, etc. etc.

I found myself branching out and adding to the hoard. I am a sewer so, using many old silks, lace and linens, I fashioned nightgowns from styles of the turn of the century. Part of my treasure trove was a cache of old picture frames. I used them to frame pictures from old magazines and they were very popular.

7th Avenue flea market

I was the only person there selling old linens out of about fifty venders, so my booth was popular with the ladies. One hot item was old cotton bags that once held fifty pounds of flour and other dry goods. I still use one myself today to roll out pastry dough.

Best of all, I made some wonderful friends and met interesting people. One was an artist, Dolores. It was her display of jewelry that first attracted me to that market. She made earrings by twisting copper wire into interesting designs. Besides jewelry, she painted in acrylic — always the same subject, mischievous little girls. Most of the people who rented a booth sold old, antique and just-used merchandise. Some, like Dolores, sold handmade jewelry and other distinctive merchandise. Almost all of the venders were retired middle-aged people. I, being 94, was the oldest — probably the oldest vender on record ever.

Artwork by Dolores Tramontano
Acrylic and silver

Early one day, a man came to my table and proceeded to pick up every item, scrutinize it and then put it down in the wrong place. After about ten minutes of this annoying fellow, I said, "Go away, come back when you have some money." He laughed and laughed and went away. It turned out the laugh was on me because the fellow was not only a vender, but one of the most liked. You might say, "The leader of the pack." Anthony and I became great friends.

The school, or its affiliate, contracted with a person who organized, ran and rented out space in the schoolyard to the venders. When their contract expired, the school had a higher bid from another vender organizer. Unfortunately, the new organizer was popular neither with the venders themselves nor the neighborhood customers. The flea market had been particularly popular for dads to take the little ones early Saturday and Sunday mornings so mommy could get a rest and the ladies would come later in the day. There were the same regular customers week after week and it was a friendly atmosphere. The regular customers shunned the new venders with their higher prices and new, rather than antique, merchandise. Gradually, after many years of camaraderie for all, the 7th Avenue flea market just faded away.

30

A Night on the Town

A feeling of exhaustion came over me as I left the theater. We had attended an Irish play with all Irish actors and my weariness was due to the fact that I did not understand a word of the dialogue because of accents of the Ole Sod, the Marlon Brando mumble-method of acting, and because of a clog in my ear trumpet. I was a prisoner for two hours in an off-Broadway seat which is not the same as a Broadway seat.

At 11:05 PM, we exited and headed for our car. Even in a city as strident as New York, it's a shock when your parking space is missing your Toyota. How can this be? Well, there's the sign right there, NO PARKING 11 PM–2 AM. 11 PM! Whoever heard of that? We're from Queens where the sidewalks and street sweepers are stashed for the night by 11 PM. The only consolation of the truth of the sign is the possibility of our having been the victim of auto theft is eliminated.

It's late and dark and cold. We accidentally stumble upon the nearest precinct and hear the bad news that Toyota has been hauled to the pound uptown someplace by the Hudson River. We find a cab. Actually, it found us. The cabby waits in that spot and nightly drives novices like us to the pound. We did not even have to tell him where to take us. The driver was an automaton.

The pound office was up a ramp in a trailer, the kind constructions crews use, except that this one had teller windows, not like those at JP Morgan Bank, but more like the kind in check-cashing places. The tellers were protected with bulletproof plexi scratched to a state of opaqueness. Yes, Toyota was there, but we could not pay the $250 and rescue her. We had to take a seat and wait until she was "processed" which took an hour and a half.

An overly fastidious person might rather stand than take a seat on one of an array of unmatched chairs with split faux leather seats and grimy backs and arms. A few of the denizens in that trailer were quite comfortable in their Naugahyde armchairs, however, and seemed to have been there permanently, kind of like a place to hang out for the quasi-homeless. Others were making a lot of noise ranting with anger and outrage at the injustice of it all. But there was a certain camaraderie among all the suffering souls and conversation flowed on all levels. One of the topics was past experiences suffered by recidivists from the trailer to their impounded Cadillacs. The pound is huge and holds acres of used cars, some are stolen vehicles, reported but never claimed. To find a car, one needs written instructions and a map with an X marks the spot. Finally, we were summoned to the window. That is a very important moment because now we find out exactly where Toyota is and how to get there.

Just as we were leaving the trailer a young liveried fellow came breathlessly in through the door. He was in a mixed state of anger and confusion. We all laughed when we saw the symbol embroidered on his shirt: UPS.

31

The Diva

It was hot in there — a small room full of people — everyone, or almost everyone, in snappy casual for the event on a summer evening. The occasion was a by-invitation-only concert. The host was providing a venue for Maria Theresa, a coloratura soprano. Programs were handed out upon entry, long enough to elicit a few groans and signs, which later turned to smiles of delight as Maria Theresa opened out.

In the audience sat the soprano's mentor and lover, Awan, relaxed in his certainty that his protégée's mellow tones would please and lull his friends from the discomfort of the sultry air. His demeanor expressed pride and contentment. His position, slightly slouched, knees crossed and with rapt attention to the presence of the soloist.

Maria Theresa was Junoesque and perfect in every aspect of her appearance. The belle époque gown of rose satin was cut on the bias to cling to her model measurements. Her dark, lustrous tresses were pulled back and coiffed in a high-arranged knot. Her long neck, raised chin and erect posture were a tableau of pure elegance. Perfect posture balanced with grace. Was it any wonder Awan loved this woman?

Everyone was captivated by Maria Theresa's voice and appearance. Any woman in the room would have died to trade places with her, except a small group of blondes, barely twenty, seated three in a row. Two were suburban Muffys, their long, straight, shiny yellow hair framing South Hampton tanned faced; two dressed in pale linens to offset their sun coloring. The third blonde, now there was a piece of machinery. Her name was Myrum. Her hair was voluminous with waves and curls everywhere undisciplined like she had just emerged from a roll in the hay. Her lips, full and glossed, moved in concert with her tendrils as she chatted with the Muffys, occasionally looking at but not seeing the vision of loveliness on the podium.

There was a tenor who filled in periodically to give Maria Theresa's vocal cords a rest, but he was only a filler and his lack of talent only made Maria Theresa's performance that more dazzling - like a bride who chooses ugly bridesmaids. His name was Niki. He not only filled in the concert gaps for Maria Theresa but filled her need for comfort and solace in bed as well.

Accompanying Maria Theresa on the piano was Grisellina, her eightieth birthday long gone but whose gnarled fingers still retained their agility. When the diva left the platform, the audience was treated to a solo by this *anciana* who captured the love and admiration of the audience. It is a miracle of life that one so worn by years could still delight the senses with her melodies. The solo signaled intermission.

Awan spared no expense for the evening. The refreshments at intermission were meant to be memorable. Many sandwiches on pita bread stuffed with meatballs of lamb and pinola nuts, or crepes stuffed with flavored onion and mint, or walnuts and roasted red peppers ground to a paste that made the tongue want to laugh and cry at the same time, all accompanied with the finest white and red wines.

The lights dimmed and Grisellina took her place and tripped out a short piece while the audience settled in, except for the two Muffys who wanted to do a bit more of the West Village before heading back to the Hamptons. Myrum remained. She was wearing a cerise velvet bustier, sequined here and there, and if there is such a phrase as "itsy bitsy" that would describe Myrum's skirt. Her ankle bracelet and gypsy jewelry completed the impression of a professional. She was exotic and sensual and now next to her, with his arm over the back of her chair, sat Awan with Myrum's tousled head resting on his shoulder, both watching Maria Theresa sing her final aria.

Not too long after the concert, they boarded a flight to Paris. Patiently awaiting his return were Maria Theresa in her chignon and Awan's wife in her hijab.

Ursula and Francesca in Prospect Park

32

Brass into Gold

I continued my education at night. After eighteen years of teaching English, I retired from the academic life and practiced law for twenty years.

As Ursula and I grew older, more independent, and financially comfortable, we laughed at the sign on a building near where we lived: Graham Home for Old Ladies, Incorporated 1851.

Seriously, the sign really says this.

Instead, we seized life and wrung out every bit of cultural advantage the city had to offer: dinners at The Rainbow Room, Top of the Sixes, Peter Luger's, Keen's Chop House, The Water Club, The River Café and ethnic meals from around the world: Arabic on Atlantic Avenue, Italian from Little Italy, Indian from East Sixth Street, China Town where our favorite was chicken feet and always seeking out real sushi all over Tinsel Town.

When we weren't savoring the world's finest culinary presentations, we were feasting our eyes on art: the ballet, museums, especially the small, privately endowed such as The Frick, The Morgan Library and Museum, The Neue Galerie, and as many art galleries as fit into our waking hours: Chelsea, Greenwich Village, Soho, Lower East Side were our haunts. On nice days, we watched the ice skaters at Rockefeller Center Rink, strolled on the High Line or in the botanical gardens. In the evenings, we enjoyed everything at Lincoln Center, small art movie theaters, flamenco performances and occasionally a Broadway show.

Nor did we neglect the dear departed. New York cemeteries were a place of interest and education for Ursula and me. Ursula was a member of the Green-Wood Historic Fund and we visited the Green-Wood Cemetery near where we lived many times. For those who have never visited the cemetery, it is recommended highly; not only for its historical site of 1776 and the Revolutionary War, but for its natural beauty.

Also to pay tribute to the many famous people, who have given us so much. Men like Elias Howe, who invented the sewing machine, is buried there, as are famous businessmen Colgate, Squib and Pfizer, and many artists like Leonard Bernstein, Jean-Michel Basquiat, Louis Comfort Tiffany, and both Currier and Ives. I would be remiss if I did not mention some of the famous gangsters who are buried at Green Wood because their monuments, statues and mausoleums are by far the most elaborate and expensive. Among those who have been so ostentatiously remembered by their survivors are "Johnny the Fox" Torrio, Alberto Anastasia and "Crazy Joe" Gallo.

Another famous graveyard to which we occasionally paid homage was the tiny, quaint Trinity Churchyard at the foot of Manhattan. It is a 1766 historical landmark where Alexander Hamilton's and Robert Fulton's graves are slowly sinking into the ground.

Ursula's photography in Prospect Park

One sad place we visited was Ellis Island, where we saw a brutal show entitled "Gulag: Soviet Forced Labor Camps and the Struggle for Freedom." It is interesting that the city put that exhibit in such a remote place, inconvenient to reach. It was a horror story. Ursula was particularly moved by it and cried when she saw the inhumane conditions her countrymen had to endure when the Russians, after invading Estonia, enslaved the men and sent them to the gulag camps where they forced the captives to build a railroad across Siberia. It made my friend emotionally drained.

A unique and memorable exhibit Ursula and I had the privilege to see was the Christo project in Central Park. The ideas of Christo and his wife Jeanne-Claude expressing their art were on a grand scale. Among the great works, Christo covered the Reichstadt in Berlin in fabric. In Paris, they wrapped the Pont Neuf, the famous bridge over the Seine. In New York, the artist came up with an entirely new idea which of course is what true artists do. They

Ursula enjoying "The Gates" in Central Park, 2005

built frames of curtains to flutter in the wind, setting the snow on fire all over the park. It should be noted that there are 843 acres in Frederick Olmsted's landscape masterpiece, 'Central Park.'

We were not always visiting cemeteries, galleries or dining. We did spend time enriching our minds. In Midtown Manhattan, there was a brownstone townhouse that had been converted into a small private college, the Henry George School of Social Sciences. After one completed the required economic courses, which taught the progressive idea of non-ownership of private property, he or she could take courses in Literature, Shakespeare, Writing and the like – all free. We took advantage of this opportunity and devoured every course we could along with other curious adults. There were some pretty lively discussions without mayhem in those days.

This is how the fates paid us back for the sordid hand we were dealt earlier. When we became too old and tired to play anymore, we retired and became just two too old *ancianas*.

At the age of 96, I retired to a lovely little storybook town in Florida, Mount Dora. Ursula was 1,000 miles away in Bradford, Pennsylvania. We corresponded until my last letter in 2019 came back "undeliverable."

Postcard by Tamla Maddox

Then, one day, I found Ursula's autobiography which she had entrusted to me. It was in my desk drawer for ten years. I thought about it and why she had left it in my care. It was to leave a message for future generations about the sufferings of war; how everything you work for can be snatched from you in a wink; how the strong overpower the weak; how cruel man is to his fellow humans; and then how one can endure devastating hardship and work his or her way out by never giving up. My dear friend, we saw the worst and the best. We, you and I, Urse, were cast in brass and we turned it to gold.

On March 5th 2023, I celebrated my 100th birthday at an elegant party given by my sweet, lovable daughter-in-law, Mary, with assistance from her family sous-chefs and my daughter Kerry, who is also a cartographer and drew the map of Estonia at the beginning of this book.

My birthday cake

Acknowledgements

I want to express my deep appreciation to Jessica Morris, my assistant, for organizing, translating, researching, typing and every other "ing" that went into preparing the pages for this book.

My publisher, Lee Sizemore, another patient soul for editing a heap of material acquired over one hundred years.

And thanks to my daughters, Kerry for preserving and organizing my pictures and for being there for me always, and Tracey for keeping me on track when I take the wrong train.

Brass, brazen youth
With salty tears
Molds to gold
In the golden years

Printed in the USA
CPSIA information can be obtained
at www.ICGtesting.com
JSHW011203051123
51235JS00015B/102